NUTSHE

INTELLECTUAL PROPERTY LAW IN A NUTSHELL

Other Titles in the Series

A Level Law
Company Law
Consumer Law
Contract Law
Constitutional and
Administrative Law
Criminal Law
Employment Law
English Legal System
Environmental Law
European Union Law
Equity and Trusts
Evidence
Family Law
Human Rights
Land Law
Medical Law
Tort
Trusts

Titles in the Nutcase Series

Constitutional and
Administrative Law
Contract Law
Criminal Law
European Union Law
Employment Law
Equity and Trusts
Human Rights
Land Law
Tort

AUSTRALIA
Law Book Company
Sydney

CANADA and USA
Carswell
Toronto

HONG KONG
Sweet & Maxwell Asia

NEW ZEALAND
Brookers
Wellington

SINGAPORE and MALAYSIA
Sweet & Maxwell Asia
Singapore and Kuala Lumpur

NUTSHELLS

INTELLECTUAL PROPERTY LAW IN A NUTSHELL

SECOND EDITION

by

CAROLINE WILSON, LL.B. (Hons) (London),
LL.M. (London).
Lecturer in Intellectual Property Law
University of Southampton

London ● Sweet & Maxwell ● 2005

Published in 2005 by Sweet & Maxwell Limited of
100 Avenue Road, London NW3 3PF
Typeset by YHT, Ltd, London
Printed in Great Britain by Creative Print & Design Group, Wales

No natural forests were destroyed to make this product.
Only farmed timber was used and re-planted.

A CIP catalogue record for this book is available from the British
Library.

ISBN 0 421 891 505

CONTENTS

1. Introduction   1
2. Remedies for IP Infringement   4
3. Patent Law   11
4. Breach of Confidence   30
5. Trade Mark Law   37
6. Passing Off   63
7. Copyright I—Subsistence of Copyright   71
8. Copyright II—Infringement, Remedies and Neighbouring Rights   81
9. Design Law   96
10. Examination Checklist   109
11. Sample Questions and Model Answers   115
12. Useful Websites   121

Index   123

1. INTRODUCTION

WHAT IS INTELLECTUAL PROPERTY?

Intellectual property (IP) is a fast-moving and sometimes complex area of law. Intellectual property rights (IPRs) is the term used to describe the various rights that afford protection to innovative and creative endeavour.

The main rights that fall within intellectual property include:

(a) Patents. A patent is a statutory property right that gives the patent owner the exclusive right to use certain inventions.

(b) Breach of confidence. The action for breach of confidence can be used to protect certain categories of confidential information (*e.g.* personal or commercial information) against unauthorised disclosure or use.

(c) Trade marks. Registered trade marks are statutory rights, and give the exclusive right to use a distinctive sign (*e.g.* a name, symbol, scent, jingle etc.) in relation to a product or service.

(d) Passing off. Goodwill is a form of property constituting the market's perception of the value and quality of a business and its products; this can be protected against interference or damage by passing off. Passing off is a tort that may be used in preventing a trader from making misrepresentations which damage the goodwill of another trader.

(e) Copyright and Moral Rights. Copyright is a statutory right subsisting in original literary, dramatic, musical and artistic works (often known as LDMA works), and, in sound recordings, films, broadcasts and the typography of published editions. Owners of copyright have a number of economic rights in their works, including the right to prevent unauthorised copying and adaptation, and there is now protection afforded to technological protection measures. There are also moral rights—rights that authors retain in their works, irrespective of who owns the economic rights.

(f) Design law. Certain functional and aesthetic aspects of the appearance of articles are protected via a combination of the registered design system, the design right (an unregistered design system) and aspects of copyright law. A registered design is the exclusive right to use certain aesthetic or functional features of a range of products. A design right is the right to prevent the copying of a functional aspect of the shape or configuration of an article such as a manufactured tool. Copyright has a residual role in the field of design law.

Further details and some of the substantive requirements of these IPRs are summarised in the table below:

Outline of Intellectual Property Rights (IPRs)

IPR	Subject Matter of the IPR	Procedure for obtaining the IPR	Duration of IPR
Patent	Novel, industrially applicable inventions capable of an inventive step	A statutory IPR obtained via application to the Patent Office	Up to 20 years
Confidential Information	Government, personal, industrial or trade secrets possessing the necessary quality of confidence	Equitable action arising via contract or the confidentiality of a relationship	Indefinite, but lasting until the information is released into the public domain
Trade Marks	Distinctive signs capable of being represented graphically	A statutory IPR obtained via application to the Trade Marks Division of the Patent Office	May be renewed indefinitely
Passing Off	Protects against misrepresentations damaging the goodwill of an enterprise	A tort	Indefinite, but lasting until the enterprise's goodwill ceases
Copyright	Literary, musical and artistic works, sound recordings, films and broadcasts etc.	A statutory IPR which arises automatically	Varies. Maximum of the life of the author plus 70 years

Moral rights	The rights to paternity and integrity, the right to object to false attribution in relation to certain copyright works. Also, the right to privacy for photographs and films	Established by statute, moral rights are personal to the author and arise automatically	The rights to paternity, integrity and privacy last for the same period as the relevant copyright. The right to object to false attribution is in place for 20 years from the death of the person subject to the false attribution
Unregistered Design Right	Functional design of articles	A statutory IPR which arises from the recording of the design	Up to 15 years
Registered Design	Aesthetic or functional aspects of the appearance of the whole or part of a product	Application to the Designs Registry of the Patent Office are required for this statutory IPR	Up to 25 years

The purpose of this text is to provide basic background on the main UK intellectual property rights but, given the importance of European institutions and laws in the IP field, reference is also made throughout to relevant European laws and decisions. For the purposes of background, therefore, it is useful to summarise the scope of the main European IP instruments that are currently in force and that are referred to elsewhere in this text:

Summary of main European IP instruments

Subject matter	European Instrument	Intended Scope or Purpose
Patent	European Patent Convention (EPC) 1973	This is an EEA, *not* an EU system, for obtaining a "bundle" of national patents
	Biotechnology Directive (98/44/EC)	Harmonises member states' laws regarding the patentability of biotechnological inventions
Trade Marks	Trade Mark Directive (89/104/EEC)	Harmonises member states' national trade mark regimes
	Trade Mark Regulation (No. 40/94)	Creates the Community Trade Mark (CTM) system
Copyright	Computer Program Directive (91/250/EEC)	Harmonises member states' copyright protection for computer programs

	Rental and Lending Rights Directive (92/100/EC)	Harmonises member states' law relating to the lending and renting of copyright works.
	Term Directive (93/98/EC)	Harmonises member states' law relating to the term of copyright
	Database Directive (96/9/EC)	Introduces a new national *sui generis* database right for database owners and harmonises aspects of member states' copyright protection for databases
	Information Society Directive (2001/29/EC)	Harmonises member states' copyright law re. the digital environment and introduces national protection of technological copy protection measures
Designs	Designs Directive (98/71/EC)	Harmonises member states' design law
	Regulation on Community Designs (No.6/2002)	Creates the Community design regime
Remedies	Enforcement directive (2004/48/EC).	Approximates national rules regarding the enforcement of IPRs

2. REMEDIES FOR IP INFRINGEMENT

INTRODUCTION

In order to be useful, IPRs must be enforced by the right-holder, so it is important to be aware of the range of civil remedies and criminal sanctions provided for the infringement of IPRs.

Generally, IP infringement involves civil remedies, but some criminal sanctions are also available. Final remedies (remedies available after trial) in practice may be less important than interim remedies (remedies awarded at the interim stage, formerly known as the interlocutory stage).

It should be noted that the EU Enforcement Directive (2004/48/EEC), which came into force on May 20, 2004, should be implemented by the UK (along with other EU member states) within two years of that date. Although it is not expected that this directive will result in fundamental change to UK law relating to IP remedies, some changes are likely to be made.

FINAL REMEDIES: PECUNIARY REMIEDIES

Financial compensation for losses caused by infringement may take the form of damages or an account of profits.

Account of profits

This is an equitable remedy involving the award to the rightholder of the profits that the defendant has made from the infringement. Account of profits is available in patent infringement (PA 1977, s.61(1)(d)), for actions for breach of confidence (see *Peter Pan v Corsets Silhouette* (1963), for trade mark infringement (TMA 1994, s.14(2)), passing off (see *My Kinda Town v Soll* (1982)), copyright infringement (CDPA 1988, s.96(2)) and infringement of the design right (CDPA 1988, s.229(2)). It is not available for infringements of registered designs. It should be noted that account of profits is a discretionary remedy and a rightholder cannot enjoy both damages and account of profits (*Potton v Yorkclose* (1990)). Where a rightholder has the choice of electing for account of profits, that choice should be an informed one (*Island Records Ltd v Tring International plc* (1995)).

In *Celanese International Corporation v BP Chemicals* (1999), guidance as how to calculate an award under account of profits was given:

(i) The first step is to ascertain the total profits possible from the activities of the infringer.
(ii) Then, if appropriate, the total profits should be apportioned to establish the ball point profit (*i.e.* the profit which is attributable to the infringement).
(iii) The resultant figure should then be adjusted to reflect the nature of the parties' cases, and
(iv) Any tax paid should then be deducted.

Damages

An award of damages is the most common pecuniary remedy for IP infringement and they are available within each IPR (although damages where there is innocent infringement, for example, may not always be available):

(a) Patent infringement (PA 1977, s.61(1)(c));
(b) Actions for breach of confidence (*e.g. Seager v Copydex (No.1)* (1967));
(c) Trade mark infringement (TMA 1994, s.14(2));
(d) Passing off;
(e) Copyright infringement (CDPA 1988, s.96(2));
(f) Infringement of design right (CDPA 1988, s.229(2)); and
(g) Registered design infringement (RDA 1949, s.9(1)).

Usually damages are calculated on the basis of lost profits or on a royalty basis. Irrespective of the method used, the general rule is that they should be compensatory; they should put the party back in the position they would have been had the infringement not occurred (*General Tire v Firestone Tyre* (1975)). It should be noted that the courts sometimes allow damages for consequential (also known as secondary or parasitic) losses (*e.g.* see *Gerber Garment Technology v Lectra Systems* (1997)).

Damages may also have a punitive element, either in the form of exemplary damages, which although theoretically available for all IPRs are rarely awarded (see the New Zealand personal injury case *A v Michael Bernard Bottrill* (2002)), or in the form of statutory additional damages. Statutory additional damages are, however, only available in copyright (CDPA 1988, s.97(2)) and for design rights (CDPA 1988, s.229(3)) and these may include a restitutionary element (*Nottinghamshire Healthcare NHS Trust v News Group Newspapers Ltd* (2002)).

FINAL REMEDIES: NON-PECUNIARY REMEDIES

(a) Declaration. Declaratory relief (a declaration of infringement or of non-infringement) is discretionary.
(b) Delivery up and destruction. In order to ensure that injunctions are properly effective, the court has the equitable power to order the delivery up of infringing articles or documents for destruction, or else to require their destruction under oath by the defendant. Delivery up may also be awarded in interim proceedings.
(c) Court order for a party to reveal relevant information. Under the Civil Procedure Rules (rule 31) such an order could be made so as to ascertain, for example, the name and address of a supplier or importer. Such orders, along with the traditional discretionary disclosure order, known as a Norwich Pharmacal order (after *Norwich Pharmacal*

(1974)) are useful to IP proprietors as they can be used to reveal the names of those that are ultimately responsible for the infringement. In recent times, concern about the use of such orders has grown; their use has implications for press freedom by undermining the tradition of maintaining the secrecy of journalists sources (although the judiciary are alive to this concern, see *e.g. Ackroyd v Mersey Care NHS Trust* (2003)) and has more general implications for freedom of expression; for example, orders for discovery have been granted against ISPs to disclose the names and addresses of an individual who have used their services (*e.g.* see *Totalise Plc v The Motely Fool Ltd and another* (2002)).

(d) Injunction. An injunction is a Court Order. They are equitable remedies given at the Court's discretion. There has been some dispute as to the appropriate breadth and the temporal and territorial scope of final injunctions; (i) appropriate breadth—the "normal" final injunction (*i.e.* not to infringe the IPR at issue) had been felt to be too vague and broad, and more specific injunctions are occasionally favoured (*Microsoft v Plato* (1999)), but the Court of Appeal has cast doubt on the appropriateness of such so-called narrow final injunctions (*Coflexip v Stolt* (2001)); (ii) the temporal scope of injunctions can vary; so-called springboard injunctions, which are limited in time, can be granted; and (iii) territorial scope—the UK courts are reluctant to award extra-territorial injunctions (*Kirin-Amgen Inc v Transkaryotic Therapies Inc (No.2)* (2002)). Injunctions are also available at the interim stage (see below).

INTERIM REMEDIES

Interim injunctions

Although an application for summary judgment can be very helpful to an IPR proprietor, an interim injunction can often provide the only effective remedy to an IP rightholder. This and the fact that most IP infringement disputes do not progress beyond the interim stage (often still referred to by the old terminology—"interlocutory stage") ensure that interim injunctions are particularly important in IP law.

The standard guidance as to when an interim injunction

should be granted was set out in *American Cyanamid v Ethicon* (1975):

(a) The claimant should have an arguable case;
(b) Damages would not provide an adequate remedy; and
(c) The courts should consider the balance of commercial convenience. If this is equal, the courts should act to preserve the *status quo*.

The *American Cyanamid* formula was criticised in *Series 5 Software v Clarke* (1996) as it was felt that interim injunctions at that time were virtually being awarded automatically; in *Series 5* the discretionary nature of interim relief and the importance of examining the merits of the case were emphasised. Despite the validity of these points, the *American Cyanamid* formula remains the test that the courts favour. This is less of a problem than might be thought, as applications for interim injunctions have decreased in recent times, as the court may instead order a speedy trial and because claimants are increasingly applying for summary judgements instead. However, one way in which the availability of interim injunctions has been reduced is in the area of human rights—due to the application of Human Rights Act 1998, s.12(3) (see *Garry Flitcroft v Mirror Group Newspapers* (2002) and *Cream Holdings and other v Banerjee and others* (2004)), in breach of confidence cases in particular. As a result, the current position on the availability of interim injunctions in breach of confidence cases where there are issues relating to freedom of expression is now somewhat more restrictive than the *American Cyanamid* formula suggests; so for such cases the guidance as to when to grant an interim injunction might be re-stated as follows:

(a) The claimant should have an arguable case except in breach of confidence cases where issues of freedom of expression are at stake; here a higher standard should apply (*Garry Flitcroft v Mirror Group Newspapers* (2002)). However, <u>what</u> that higher standard should be is now unclear. In *Flitcroft* it was suggested that "the claimant being likely to succeed at trial" was the appropriate test. However, the House of Lords in *Cream Holdings and other v Banerjee and others* (2004) has ruled that one should instead "consider whether the applicant's prospects of success at trial are sufficiently favourable to justify such an order being made in the particular circumstances of the case";

(b) Damages would not provide an adequate remedy; and

(c) The courts should consider the balance of commercial convenience. If this is equal, the courts should act to preserve the *status quo*. In breach of confidence cases where an issue of freedom of expression is at stake, as per *Garry Flitcroft v Mirror Group Newspapers* (2002), the court should weigh up the claim based on freedom of expression as against the claimant's position. If, as in *Garry Flitcroft v Mirror Group Newspapers* (2002), the claimant invokes a claim of privacy, the court should weigh the claim to privacy as against that of the claim to freedom of expression and an injunction should only be granted here where it is justified.

Ex parte orders

Inter partes proceedings (now known as proceedings on notice) are proceedings where the defendant has been served and has had sufficient time to prepare his defence. In contrast, *ex parte* hearings (now known as proceedings without notice) is a hearing where only one side is represented (as per *Intergraph v Solid Systems* (1993), this party is under a duty of full and frank disclosure). *Ex parte* orders preserve the *status quo* pending a full hearing. There are two such orders which are of relevance:

(a) Search orders. These were formerly known as Anton Piller Orders after *Anton Piller* (1976), the case where the first such order was granted. Most of the guidelines for and safeguards against the abuse of search orders are now codified in the Civil Procedure Rules (Practice Direction 25); for example, the applicant must be able to demonstrate a strong *prima facie* case of infringement. There must also be a likelihood of real and serious damage, clear evidence that there are documents or property at the alleged infringer's site and a serious possibility that they will be destroyed if the alleged infringer is put on notice. Other safeguards include that the order must be carried out by an experienced independent solicitor, where documents are removed they must be returned within two days and, where possible, the order must be carried out on business premises during business hours. The grant of a search order allows the premises of an alleged infringer to be searched and evidence of infringement to be seized. The courts have developed safeguards against the abuse of search orders (*Universal Thermosensors v Hibben* (1992)).

(b) Freezing injunction. These were formerly known as Mareva injunctions. These injunctions freeze the assets of an alleged infringer pending a full trial (*Mareva* (1975)), thus preventing the alleged infringer from transferring assets out of the jurisdiction. The guidelines relating to the availability of freezing injunctions have been codified under the Civil Procedure Rules (Practice Direction 25), but it should be noted that there are fewer safeguards against the abuse of freezing injunctions than there are in relation to search orders.

CRIMINAL SANCTIONS

Generally, IP infringement involves civil remedies, but some criminal sanctions are available and criminal liability and sanctions are particularly important in relation to piracy and counterfeiting activities. Applicable criminal sanctions can be found outside intellectual property law, *e.g.* the Trade Descriptions Act 1968, and the law student should be generally aware of this. Attention, however, should be paid to the statutory IP criminal sanctions (please note that criminal sanctions for *infringement* only exist in copyright law and trade mark law):

(a) Patents (PA 1977, ss.109 and 110);
(b) Trade marks (TMA 1994, ss.59, 60, 92);
(c) Copyright (CDPA 1988, ss.107–10, 198, 297, 297A, 296ZB and 201); and
(d) Registered designs (RDA 1949, ss.35 and 35A).

THREATS

Groundless threats to sue for IP infringement may in themselves be actionable where there is relevant statutory protection, see:

(a) PA 1977, s.70 (please note that this section has recently been amended, e.g. PA 1977, s.70(2)(A) provides a new defence to a threats action);
(b) TMA 1994, s.21; and
(c) RDA 1949, s.26.

In IPRs where the threats action is available, because of some differences in the statutory drafting, it may be that the rules vary as between different IP rights. However, in general the claimant needs to establish that an actionable threat was made and that they were aggrieved by this threat. Provided that the defendant cannot demonstrate that the threat was justified (*i.e.* there has been a groundless threat), the claimant is entitled to the relief specified in the relevant statutory provisions.

3. PATENT LAW

INTRODUCTION

What is a patent?

Patents are monopoly rights. Products or processes may be patented but irrespective of the form of the patent, the product or process must satisfy the substantive criteria of the Patents Act 1977 (PA 1977). These are:

(i) Restrictions as to subject-matter. There must be an *invention*, but *not an "as such" inventions or non-patentable inventions* (PA 1977, ss.1(2) 1(3) and Sch.A2, para.3);
(ii) *Novelty* must be present (PA 1977, s.2);
(iii) An *inventive step* must be present (PA 1977, s.3); and
(iv) The invention must be capable of *industrial application* (PA 1977, s.4).

It should be noted that the Patents Act 2004 (PA 2004) was granted Royal Assent on July 22, 2004; the PA 2004 is being implemented in several stages, so the student should be aware that a number of amendments to the PA 1977 can be expected over the next few years (this text reflects patent law at the time of writing).

OBTAINING A PATENT

A patent is a territorial right, so it is necessary to apply for a patent in each jurisdiction for which protection is desired, *e.g.* a

UK patent may be obtained from the UK Patent Office. There is currently no EU patent system (a single patent valid in all EU member states), although the EU has legislated on patent law (*e.g.* the Biotechnology Directive (98/44/EC)). However, a "bundle" of national patents from states that are party to the European Patent Convention 1973 (EPC) may be obtained from a single patent application to the European Patent Office (EPO); somewhat confusingly, patents obtained via the EPC route are termed "European patents". In fact, one should be aware that there are three main routes to acquiring patent protection valid in the UK:

(i) The national route (*i.e.* an application for a UK patent);
(ii) The EPC route (PA 1977, ss.77 and 78. *i.e.* an application for a "European patent", a bundle of national patent rights. Applicants have to designate the EPC member states in which they wish to obtain protection); and
(iii) The Patent Cooperation Treaty 1970 (PCT) route (PA 1977, s.89. The PCT offers an international patent filing system, which expedites the process of applying for a patent in PCT member states; it is ultimately for each designated member state, however, to decide whether a national patent is granted).

Because of the importance of the EPC route to acquiring patent protection, the fact that the PA 1977 is based on the EPC 1973, and because they are regarded as being persuasive authorities in the UK for PA 1977, ss.1–4, EPO decisions ("EPO *decision*" is the correct terminology—it is misleading to speak of "EPO *cases*"; the EPO is not a court) are relevant to UK patents. With this fact in mind, the reader might find the table below, which presents some of key provisions relating to the substantive criteria of patentability under the PA 1977 with the equivalent provisions under the EPC, useful:

Main substantive patentability requirements under PA 1977 and EPC 1973

	UK Patents Act 1977	European Patent Convention 1973
Patentability requirements (general)	s.1(1)	Art.52

Subject matter (various)		
Things, not inventions "as such"	s.1(2)	Art.52(2)(3)
Non-patentable inventions—immoral inventions and inventions contrary to public policy	s.1(3) (see also para.3 Sch.A2)	Art.53(a)
Non-patentable inventions—certain biological subject matter	Para.3(f) Sch.A2	Art.53(b)
Novelty (PA 1977, s.2/EPC 1973, Arts 54 and 55)		
Definition of novelty	s.2(1)	Art.54(1)
Scope of the state of the art	ss.2(2) and 2(3)	Art.54.(2)–(5)
Limited grace period	s.2(4)	Art.55
Novelty of first medical uses	s.2(6)	Art.54(5)
Inventive step (PA 1977, s.3/EPC, Art.56)		
Industrial Application (PA 1977, s.4/EPC, Art.52(1)–(4))		
Definition of industrial application	s.4(1)	Art.57
Exceptions to industrial applications	s.4(2)	Art.52(4)

THINGS, NOT INVENTIONS "AS SUCH"

Although *Genetech v Wellcome* (1989) teaches us that patents will only be granted where the applicant has made an invention, the statute does not provide a definition of "invention"; instead PA 1977, s.1(2) sets out a list of things that are considered not to be inventions "as such" (this list perhaps constituting a *negative definition* of invention).

Generally, abstract, aesthetic and non-technical things are considered to be excluded things "as such". Determining whether a thing constitutes excluded subject matter "as such" under PA 1977, s.1(2) can be complex—and there is not always a consistent approach to this issue. As will be seen below, for s.1(2)(c), the concept of technical contribution is used to determine whether a thing constitutes a computer program "as such", but some commentators consider that the concept of technical contribution should now be applied to all excluded things under PA 1977, s.1(2).

You should appreciate the fundamental legal distinction between PA 1977, s.1(2) and PA 1977, s.1(3)—where a patent application fails on the basis of PA 1977, s.1(2), *the subject matter has not reached the threshold of "invention"* (if you like, it is a "sub-invention"), but where a patent application fails on s.1(3), here, the subject matter is an invention, but is a *non-patentable invention*).

Discoveries, scientific theories and mathematical methods

Discoveries, scientific theories and mathematical methods are not inventions "as such" (PA 1977, s.1(2)(a)). It has been suggested that a discovery is a disclosure that adds to the amount of human knowledge, whereas an invention necessarily also suggests an act to be done (*Reynolds v Smith* (1913)). The line between discovery and invention can be difficult to draw, but it is clear that a "mere" discovery must be developed and applied in some way before it constitutes an invention. Therefore, finding a naturally-occurring compound in the human body would be considered to be a discovery, but processes used to isolate or purify such a compound or a synthetic version of the naturally-occurring compound would be inventions.

Similar principles hold true for scientific theories and mathematical methods; on their own they are unpatentable, but where they are developed or applied in some way, as is suggested in *Fujitsu Ltd's Application* (1997) where they make a technical contribution, they will be patentable.

Aesthetic creations

Literary, dramatic, musical and artistic works or any other aesthetic creation are not inventions "as such" (PA 1977, s.1(2)(b)); this provision rarely causes difficulties and the rationale for this exception is that such subject matter is already protected by copyright and, by its nature, is not technical.

Computer programs

PA 1977, s.1(2)(c) lists a number of things that are not regarded as being inventions "as such", and one of the most problematic things included in this list is computer programs. The most important matter to bear in mind is that despite s.1(2)(c), patents for software-related inventions are in fact granted. Software-related patents will be granted where a *substantive technical contribution* is made (this concept derives from a line of EPO decisions from *VICOM/Computer-related invention* (1987), onwards) as this is not considered to be a computer program "as such". In deciding whether there is a technical contribution, one of two approaches may be taken:

(a) One should ask whether technical means are used to produce a result or solve a problem; or

(b) One should ask whether the invention produces a technical result.

Although there has been some UK criticism of the substantive technical contribution approach (*e.g.* see *Fujitsu Ltd's Application* (1977)), the UK does take into account the EPO's jurisprudence on the patentability of software-related inventions, so students should use the technical contribution approach. Nevertheless, it must be said that it is generally believed that a software-related patent application is more likely to succeed before the EPO under the EPC 1973, than in the UK under the PA 1977. It should therefore be noted that if the EU Commission succeeds in implementing a Computer Programs directive (at present, a draft directive is under discussion), this would almost certainly mean that the UK would have to take a more liberal approach to the patentability of software-related inventions.

A scheme, rule or method for performing a mental act, playing a game or business methods

The following are not patentable "as such" (PA 1977, s.1(2)(c)):

(i) Mental acts. Although UK case law in this area is limited, it does appear that the UK courts take a much stricter approach to this exclusion than does the EPO. In *Raytheon's Application* (1993) the claim was held to be excluded as it was merely an automation of a method normally carried out by individuals, *i.e.* for the UK courts this was a mental act "as such". Carrying out this method with a computer did not involve a technical contribution, even though computer automation made the process much faster and, presumably, more reliable. In contrast, the EPO has a more generous approach (see *IBM/text clarity processing* (1990)) to automated mental acts; although (as with the UK) a mental act itself is not patentable, where a mental act is carried out by a technical process (*e.g.* an automated mental act that is much quicker and more accurate than the non-automated mental act), there will be a technical contribution, and that technical process may be patentable. It should be noted that, in practice, most modern automated mental acts will involve a computer program;

(ii) Schemes, rules or methods for playing a game. It is difficult to see how innovations in this area could be said to be making a technical contribution. For example, a blue coloured squash ball might add desirable characteristics to play such as enhanced visual impact and thus a competitive advantage (the facts of *ITS Rubber* (1979), where the claim was allowed; but it should be noted that this case was decided under the Patents Act 1949), but such an advantage might not amount to a technical contribution under the current UK patent regime; and

(iii) Business methods. The UK courts have traditionally taken a strict approach to the patentability of business methods—inventions must make a technical contribution but that contribution must not be in an excluded thing (such as a business method), and, in any case, advances in the field of business are not technical (*Merill Lynch's Application* (1989)). However, the EPO's approach to business methods is less consistent. It appears that the EPO takes a more relaxed approach to business methods; in *SOHEI/General-purpose management system* (1996) the EPO indicated that "business" should be construed narrowly. Further, the implication of the EPO's decision in *PBS PARTNERSHIP/ Pension Benefits System* (2001) ("a computer suitably programmed for use in a particular field, even business is a concrete apparatus as in a physical entity, man-made for a utilitarian purpose and is therefore an invention") is that while *process claims* to business methods are not inventions "as such", *product claims* may be patentable. This is, in the view of this author, a spurious distinction, but it does mean that method claims to business methods to the EPO can be "dressed up" as product claims and thus escape the business method exclusion (the UK rejects this spurious distinction, *e.g.* see *Hutchins' Application* (2002)).

It should be noted that, in practice, many modern business methods also involve the use of computer programs.

The presentation of information

PA 1977, s.1(2)(d) provides that means of presenting information are not inventions "as such". Nevertheless, the EPO's decision in *KONINKLIJKE PHILIP'S ELECTRONICS/Picture-retrieval system* (2000) indicates that this exclusion is now interpreted narrowly; where information is functional in nature, there is deemed to be a technical contribution and it may be patentable. This is an area lacking clarity; the EPO's guidelines for discerning when information can be said to be functional are not, in the opinion of this author, clear, and it is also unclear as to whether UK courts will follow EPO jurisprudence here.

NON-PATENTABLE INVENTIONS

There are currently two categories of non-patentable inventions and these are set out below.

Inventions contrary to public policy or morality

In the rare circumstances where the commercial exploitation of an invention would be contrary to public policy or morality, that invention would be unpatentable (PA 1977, s.1(3)); the incitement to riot or to engage in criminal acts or grossly obscene matter would be examples of subject matter contrary to public policy or morality. There is a dearth of recent UK case law in this area, but the EPO's decision in *HARVARD/Onco-Mouse* (1991) demonstrates that morality and public policy should be addressed via a utilitarian balancing exercise. For example, in the *Onco-Mouse* decision itself, the EPO considered that the suffering of the onco-mouse and the possible environmental risks posed by the genetically modified mouse were outweighed by other factors, including the utility of the invention as an aid to cancer research to humans; hence the onco-mouse was not immoral. There is, not unexpectedly, disagreement among commentators as to how public policy and morality *should* be judged in the patent system, but most agree that morality is *actually* judged via the *Onco-Mouse* balancing exercise (despite the fact that the decision in *PLANT GENETIC SYSTEMS/Glutamine synthetase inhibitors* (1995) is somewhat out of step with the *Onco-Mouse* approach; here a Natural Law approach to morality, rather than a utilitarian approach, was used).

PA 1977, s.1(4) makes it clear that an invention being illegal under UK law is not, in itself, sufficient to deem an invention as being contrary to public policy or morality.

Because of the specific concerns of public policy and morality relating to genetic engineering, PA 1977, Sch.A2 provides guidance on biotechnological inventions that are contrary to PA 1977, s.1(3):

(i) PA 1977, Sch.A2 para.3(b) provides that human cloning processes are not patentable inventions.

(ii) PA 1977, Sch.A2 para.3(c) provides that processes for modifying human germ line genetic identity, *i.e.* genetic changes that can be passed to the next generation, are not patentable inventions.

(iii) PA 1977, Sch.A2 para.3(e) specifically provides that that genetic engineering of animals which is likely to cause the animal to suffer without a substantial medical benefit, either to man or animals, does not constitute a patentable invention.

Certain biological subject matter

PA 1977, Sch.A2 (which implements the Biotechnology directive (98/44/EC)) provides that although biological products and processes are not, *per se*, unpatentable, certain biological subject matter cannot constitute patentable inventions. The most important exclusions here are:

(a) Animal or plant varieties or essentially macrobiological processes (PA 1977, Sch.A2 para.3(f)). It should be noted that:

(i) Although animal and plant varieties are not, *per se*, patentable, in practice because of the EPO's very narrow definitions of *"variety"*, careful drafting of patent claims can help the patent applicant avoid this prohibition. According to the EPO, an *animal variety* is a species or a sub-unit of an animal species, and the EPO's definition of a *plant variety* is to be found in PA 1977, Sch.A2 para.11 ("... a plant grouping within a single botanical taxon of the lowest known rank ..."). This means that where the invention is *not confined to a particular variety*, it may be patented (*HARVARD/Onco-Mouse (1991) and NOVARTIS/Transgenic Plant (1999)*). Therefore, a claim that related to *Rattus norvegicus* (the common laboratory rat) would be caught by this exclusion, but the same technology claimed for non-human mammals would not. Similarly, a claim that related to *Triticum monococcum* (cultivated Einkorn wheat) would be caught by this exclusion, but the same technology claimed for the entire genus *Triticum* (this includes, for example, common wheat, durum wheat, spelt and wild emmer) would not. UK practice has followed EPO practice here.

(ii) The distinction between a microbiological or technical process (which would be patentable) and a macrobiological process (which would not be patentable) is not entirely clear, but microbiological processes have been said to be processes using micro-organisms to make or modify products (*PLANT GENETIC SYSTEMS/Glutamine synthetase inhibitors* (1995). See also PA 1977, Sch.A2 para.11).

(b) The formation and development of the human body and mere discoveries of elements of the human body (this includes gene sequences) are not patentable inventions. However, where a *technical process* is used to isolate or produce elements (including genes) from the human body, this may be patentable (PA 1977, Sch.A2 para.3(a)); and

NOVELTY

An invention must be novel (PA 1977, s.1(1)(a)). In patent law, the terms *novelty* and *anticipation* are used interchangeably.

The novelty test

The invention must be new in the sense that it must not previously have been made available to the public. PA 1977, s.2(1) provides that an invention is novel where it does not form part of the state of the art.

Novelty is judged by asking *is the invention part of the state of the art?* and implicitly this statutory test has two aspects: (i) has there been a disclosure?, and (ii) is that disclosure sufficient to anticipate the invention?

In practice, an enquiry into novelty tends to be phrased differently to this, with different terminology being used depending on whether the invention at issue is a product or a process.

Therefore, after referring to the statutory test in PA 1977, s.2(1), one should expand on this as follows; in order for an invention to be anticipated, the prior art must either contain an *enabling disclosure* (*Evans Medical Ltd's Patent* (1998)) in the case of a product patent, or, for process patents it must give *clear and unmistakable directions to do what the applicant has invented* (*General Tire* (1972)). Novelty is, essentially, a factual issue and it is assessed objectively—UK and EPO practice on novelty are very similar.

The state of the art

PA 1977, s.2(2) defines the state of the art as comprising all matter made available to the public before the priority date of the invention (the priority date is the date of the first patent application). It therefore comprises all knowledge (worldwide) on the subject matter of the invention.

The state of the art includes matter included in earlier patent applications, including those patent applications that are not yet published (PA 1977, s.2(3)). Everything in the state of the art is known as "prior art" and the mode of disclosure is irrelevant. Novelty-destroying prior art could include, for example, information that is part of common general knowledge (*e.g. Buhler v Satake* (1997)), information disclosed via prior use (*e.g. Windsurfing v Tabor Marine* (1985)), or information disclosed in the form of a single copy of a document (publication) or via oral disclosure. Earlier patent applications published on or after the priority date also form part of the state of the art (PA 1977, s.2(2)), however, where information has been disclosed in breach of confidence (PA 1977, ss.2(4)(a) and (b)) or the invention has been displayed at an international exhibition (PA 1977, s.2(4)(c)), such disclosures are deemed not to be novelty-destroying for a six-month period.

Novel new uses

In some circumstances, a known invention may still be patented where a new use is found for it:

(a) First medical use. The PA 1977 provides that the first medical use of a known compound is novel, provided that the medical application of the compound does not itself form part of the state of the art (PA 1977, s.2(6));

(b) Second and subsequent medical use. In Europe, a practice has developed of also allowing the patenting of second and subsequent medical uses of known compounds (*EISAI/Second Medical Indication* (1985)). Such claims are deemed to be novel where the second or subsequent medical use does not form part of the state of the art, and, provided the patent application itself takes a very narrow form known as a Swiss Form claim, *i.e.* the patent claim must follow the formula "use of substance X for the manufacture of a medicine for the treatment of Disease Y". The UK courts have sanctioned the use of Swiss Form claims, but second and subsequent medical uses will only be novel in the UK where there is a new therapeutic application; merely discovering further information about a known medical use is insufficient (*Bristol-Myers Squibb v Baker Norton Pharmaceuticals* (2001)); and

(c) Second (non-medical) use. It is also possible for new uses of known things to be novel in the non-medical field where they are directed towards a new use that is sufficiently different so as not to be regarded as being part of the state of the art. This is assessed by asking: "has the claimed functional technical feature previously been made available to the public?" (*MOBIL/ Friction Reducing Additive* (1990)). In *MOBIL*, a compound previously used as a rust-preventing additive was successfully patented for use for the purpose of reducing friction. The friction-reducing qualities of the compound were the functional technical feature and as the compound has only previously been known and used for rust-prevention, this use was novel. *MOBIL*-type reasoning is recognised in the UK but has, nevertheless, been subject to some criticism (*e.g.* in *Merrill Dow v Norton* (1996)).

INVENTIVE STEP

A patentable invention must involve an inventive step; an inventive step is present where the invention would not be obvious to a person skilled in the art (PA 1977, s.3). In patent law, the terms *inventive step* and *non-obviousness* are used interchangeably.

Inventive step is a very different question from that of novelty. For the purposes of inventive step, the relevant prior art (*i.e.* the state of the art) is slightly different from as that for novelty (see above); unpublished patent applications do not form part of the state of the art for the purposes of inventive step (PA 1977, s.3). More fundamentally, inventive step is a *qualitative* question as opposed to the *quantitative* nature of novelty.

The skilled man

Inventive step are assessed from the perspective of the person skilled in the art (PA 1977, s.3)—the skilled man. This notional figure has certain attributes: he is the average person in the relevant art, possessing the relevant skills, knowledge and qualifications (*Technograph Printed Circuits v Mills* (1972)). Where research in the relevant art would be carried out by a research team, the viewpoint of the notional research team will instead be adopted (*Genetech Inc's Patent* (1989)). There is some questioning as to whether the skilled man is entirely uninventive (*e.g.* Mustill L.J. and Purchase L.J. in *Genetech* (1989)), but it would seem that that is indeed the case (*PLG Research v Ardon International* (1995)).

The Windsurfer test

The statutory test for inventive step has been structured into what is known as the *Windsurfer* test; this test follows the approach set out in *Windsurfing v Tabur Marine* (1985), as modified by *PLG Research Ltd v Ardon International Ltd* (1995). According to the *Windsurfer* test, in order to assess obviousness one should ask:

(i) What is the inventive step involved in the patent?
(ii) At the priority date, what was the state of the art relevant to that step?
(iii) How does the step differ from the state of the art?
(iv) Without hindsight, would the taking of that step be obvious to the person skilled in the art?

There are two ways in which one could question the importance of the *Windsurfer* test to UK patent law and these are set out below. Yet, this should not detract from the fact that *Windsurfer* continues to be primary test for inventive step in the UK:

(a) The structured approach of the *Windsurfer* test was considered by the Court of Appeal in *David John Instance v Denny Bros. Printing Ltd.* (2001) to be useful, but not essential to the inventive step enquiry; and

(b) The EPO uses a very different approach to inventive step, the problem and solution approach, and the occasional commentator has suggested that the UK should consider using the EPO approach instead. The UK courts have not shown any enthusiasm for this suggestion, but students should be generally aware of the three questions that comprise the EPO's problem and solution approach to inventive step:
   (i)   Determine the closest prior art;
   (ii) Establish the technical problem to be solved; and
   (iii) Consider whether or not the claimed invention, starting from the closest prior art and the technical problem, would have been obvious (at the priority date) to the skilled man.

It should be noted that the scope of the state of the art is narrower for inventive step than it is for novelty (PA 1977, s.3); earlier patent applications (PA 1977, s.2(3)) do not form part of the state of the art for the inventive step enquiry.

Secondary considerations

Some things are clearly obvious, *e.g.* a collocation (a combination of two known machines with no resultant improvement in function) will be obvious (*Williams v Nye* (1890)). Assessment of obviousness is often more difficult, however, and other tests may be useful. Where other obviousness tests are used with *Windsurfer*, they are known as secondary considerations and the correct use of secondary considerations is in a supplementary role, informing the fourth element of the *Windsurfer* test (*Mölnlycke AB v Procter & Gamble Ltd (No.1)* (1990)).

A number of obviousness tests have been used as secondary considerations over the years, *e.g.* has the inventor done something unexpected (*Mutoh Industry's Application* (1984)) or, if it is obvious to try, why has it not been done before (*Lucas v Gaedor* (1978)), but the following are probably the most relevant secondary considerations in modern patent law:

(i) Commercial success. The relevance of commercial success to obviousness was traditionally doubted, as commercial success can flow from factors other than inventiveness (*e.g.* advertising). However, the commercial success of the invention may now be a material factor in determining whether the new result was obvious or not (*Haberman v Jackal International* (1999)), particularly where that invention meets a long-felt want; and

(ii) The "obvious to try" test (*John Manville's Patent* (1967)) asks whether, at the priority date, the invention was worth trying and whether there was reasonable expectation of beneficial results. More recently, in *Saint-Gobain PAM SA v Fusion Provida Limited and others* (2004) it was noted that something is obvious to try when it is self-evident to the unimaginative man skilled in the art.

INDUSTRIAL APPLICATION

The invention must be capable of being applied in industry (PA 1977, s.4). Virtually all inventions bar those that are theoretically impossible (*e.g.* perpetual motion machines) can be said to meet this requirement; it is the exclusions to industrial applicability that can cause difficulties.

At present, the PA 1977 (rather artificially) deems that methods of treatment of the human or animal body including surgery, therapy or diagnosis are capable of industrial application (PA 1977, s.4(2)). As substances or equipment used in medical treatment are deemed to be capable of industrial application (PA 1977, s.4(3)), this leads to the distinction between methods of medical and veterinary treatment (which are not patentable) and products used in such treatments (which will potentially be patentable). So, an anaesthetic drug and anaesthetic equipment might be patentable but the dosage regime employed in using the anaesthetic drug and surgical techniques would not be patentable.

OWNERSHIP OF PATENTS AND THE EMPLOYEE INVENTOR

The basic rules are that a patent may be granted to the following:

(i) The inventor or joint inventors, *i.e.* the actual deviser(s) of the invention (PA 1977, s.7(2)(a));

(ii) The inventor(s)' successors in title; or

(iii) The employer of an employee inventor (see below).

Ownership of employee inventions

Inventors have the right to be mentioned as such in published patent applications and any patent granted (PA 1977, s.13), and the rebuttable assumption is that the inventor is the first owner (PA 1977, s.7(4)); but PA 1977, s.39(1) provides for a significant exception to this—where inventors are employees (see PA 1977, s.130), their employer will be the first owner of the invention if:

(a) The invention was made in the course of the employee's normal duties (*e.g. Harris' Patent* (1985)) or in the course of specially assigned duties, provided he/she might reasonably be expected to carry those duties out (*e.g. Electrolux v Hudson* (1977)); or

(b) Where the employee has a special obligation to further the interests of his employer's undertaking. This is related to the duty of fidelity that employees owe their employers; typically, the more senior the employee, the greater the scope of this obligation and the more likely that the invention belongs to the employer.

Compensation for employee inventors

Where the invention belongs to the employer (PA 1977, s.39(1)), statutory compensation of the employee inventor may be available (PA 1977, s.40), provided that:

(i) The patent is of outstanding benefit to the employer.
(ii) The invention is subject of a patent grant, and
(iii) It is just that compensation to be awarded.

The threshold for statutory compensation is very high and there has never been a reported case where statutory compensation under the PA 1977 has been awarded (such disputes tend to be settled out of court).

SUFFICIENCY

Patent applications may fail or granted patents subsequently may be revoked (PA 1977, s.72(1)(c)) on the basis of sufficiency. A patent application has a number of components and the patent specification is a vital part in which the invention is described and defined, it is the source of all the information about the patent that reached the public domain.

The specification must disclose the invention in such a way that the invention could be performed by the person skilled in the art (PA 1977, s.14(3)), *i.e.* the application must contain an enabling disclosure (*Biogen v Medeva* (1997)).

Patent claims themselves determine the scope of the monopoly granted to a patent proprietor. Claims must be clear and concise, be supported by the description and relate to a single inventive concept (PA 1977, s.14(5)).

INFRINGEMENT

The following activities carried out in the UK without the consent of the patent proprietor constitute patent infringement:

(a) Primary infringement. This falls into three categories:
   (i) PA 1977, s.60(1)(a), where a *product patent* is at issue, making, disposing of, offering to dispose of, using, importing or keeping the patented product (for disposal or otherwise).
   (ii) PA 1977, s.60(1)(b), where a *process patent* is at issue, use of the process with actual or constructive knowledge that non-consensual use constitutes infringement.
   (iii) PA 1977, s.60(1)(c). The use, offer to dispose of, importation or keeping (for disposal or otherwise) of a product directly obtained from a patented process. However, where intermediate steps are necessary the defendant's product will not infringe the claimant's process patent (*Pioneer Electronics v Warner Music Manufacturing* (1995)).
(b) Contributory infringement (s.60(2)). The supply or offer to supply any of the means that relate to an essential element of the invention, for putting the invention into effect may constitute infringement. This will only be the case where there is actual or constructive knowledge that these means are suitable (and are intended) for putting the invention into effect in the UK.

Proceedings for patent infringement may be brought by the exclusive licensee as well as by the patent proprietor (PA 1977, s.67(1)).

Exceptions to Infringement

There are a number of exceptions to patent infringement set out in PA 1977, s.60(5)(a)–(f). The main exceptions are:

(a) Private and non-commercial use (PA 1977, s.60(5)(a)).
(b) Experimental use (PA 1977, s.60(5)(b)).

The courts have considered whether repairs to patented products constitute patent infringement a number of times. The position (as set out in *British Leyland v Armstrong* (1986)) is relatively clear; genuine repair of a patented product that has been sold for use with the consent of the proprietor does not constitute infringement, only repair that amounts to reconstruction will infringe. The boundary between making a product (which constitutes infringement) and repairing a product (which falls outside) is to be judged objectively (*United Wire Ltd v Screen Repair Services (Scotland) Ltd & Another* (2001)).

Finally, there are limited prior user rights. A person who made use of an invention before its priority date may continue to use that invention, subject to certain restrictions (PA 1977, s.64).

Counterclaim for revocation

An opponent can attack a patent by counterclaiming for revocation of the patent. The grounds for revocation are:

(i) Not a patentable invention PA 1977, s.72(1)(a)), *i.e.* the subject matter of the patent is not an invention "as such" or the invention is contrary to public policy or morality, or has been anticipated; is obvious or is not industrially applicable;
(ii) Non-entitlement (PA 1977, s.72(1)(b)). The person granted the patent is not the person entitled to the patent;
(iii) Insufficiency (PA 1977, s.72(1)(c)). The patent specification does not amount to an enabling disclosure; or
(iv) Impermissible amendment (PA 1977, s.72(1)(d) and (e)). The protection afforded by the patent has been extended by an amendment that should not have been allowed.

Claim Interpretation

To establish infringement, the allegedly infringing act must fall within the scope of the patent claims. This can be difficult to determine where the allegedly infringing product or process is a variant of the patented product or process, and much patent litigation therefore focuses on claim interpretation; the process of determining the scope of a patent. Because PA 1977, s.125 requires compliance with the Protocol to the Interpretation of EPC 1973, Art.69, patent claims should be interpreted not in a strict literal way, nor in such a way that the patent claims are viewed as mere guidelines, but a position should be adopted between these two extremes so as to ensure fairness for the patentee and certainty for third parties.

It is not entirely certain as to whether the UK's approach to claim interpretation, the purposive approach (first stated in *Catnic Components v Hill Smith* (1982) and reworked in *Improver Corporation v Consumer Products* (1990)), is consistent with the Protocol (*e.g.* see *PLG Research v Ardon International Ltd* (1995)). The purposive approach (*Catnic* as restated in *Improver*) is as follows:

(i) Had the variant a material effect on the manner in which the invention works?
(ii) If not, would this have been obvious?
(iii) If yes, would the reader understand that strict compliance with the wording of the invention was required by the patentee?
(iv) If yes, the variant is outside the claim.

There have been, and continue to be, a number of debates relating to the purposive approach to claim interpretation, for example:

(i) There were some questions as to whether the purposive approach to claim interpretation was consistent with the Protocol to the Interpretation of EPC 1973, Art.69 (*e.g.* see *PLG Research v Ardon International Ltd* (1995)). However, following *Kirin-Amgen Inc and others v Hoechst Marion Roussel Limited and others* (2004), where the House of Lords stated that the purposive approach is consistent with the Protocol, this issue seems to be settled;
(ii) It is not helpful that the third element of the purposive test

has often been applied in an inconsistent manner (*e.g.* see the varying approaches employed by the judges in *Wheatley v Drillsafe* (2001)); and

(iii) There has been some debate as to whether a US patent law doctrine—"the doctrine of equivalents" is applicable in UK patent law. However, the House of Lords have addressed this question (*Kirin-Amgen Inc and others v Hoechst Marion Roussel Limited and others* (2004)) and concluded that no, the doctrine of equivalents is not applicable.

Remedies

Remedies are discussed in general in Chapter 2. The following remedies are available for patent infringement:

(i) Injunction (PA 1977, s.61(1)(a)).
(ii) An order for delivery up or destruction (PA 1977, s.61(1)(b)).
(iii) Damages *or* account of profits (PA 1977, s.61(1)(c) and (d)), but no damages or account shall be ordered where the infringer had no reasonable grounds for supposing that the patent existed (PA 1977, s.62(1)).
(iv) Declaration that the patent is valid and not infringed (PA 1977 s.61(1)(e)).

A declaration, injunction and damages are also available where a groundless threat of patent infringement (PA 1977, s.70)) is made.

CRIMINAL SANCTIONS

Provision for criminal sanctions is made in PA 1977, ss.110–111.

4. BREACH OF CONFIDENCE

INTRODUCTION

The action for breach of confidence has its origins in equity (*Naomi Campbell v Mirror Group Newspapers* (2004)). It can operate as a supplementary action, supporting as an action for patent infringement for example, or it can form an action by itself. The law of confidence protects all qualifying confidences in the private, governmental and commercial arenas, but different policy considerations are likely to affect the scope of protection within each of these three "categories" of confidential information.

Privacy—the impact of the Human Rights Act 1998

Traditionally, there was no right to privacy in the UK (*Kaye v Robertson* (1991)). With the introduction of the Human Rights Act (HRA) 1998, English law now recognises the right to privacy in accordance with European Convention on Human Rights (ECHR), Art.8 (this was first explicitly stated in *Douglas v Hello!* (2001)). This right must, however, be balanced against European Convention on Human Rights, Art.10 which guarantees freedom of expression (*Douglas v Hello!* (2001)).

It is vital to appreciate that although there is now a *right of privacy* in the UK, there is *no cause of action in privacy* (*Secretary of State for the Home Department v Wainwright* (2001)); the right to privacy is instead enforced via a range of causes of action, breach of confidence being chief among them, and there is now a significant and growing body of breach of confidence cases that concern privacy issues. Whether there *should* be a tort of privacy is, of course, another issue (and a hotly debated one, at that). Where breach of confidence cases concern ECHR, Art.8, the elements of the action for breach of confidence, of course, have to be made out (see the following sections of Chapter 4), but the following points also should be borne in mind:

(a) There are differing degrees of privacy (as acknowledged in the Court of Appeal's interim decision in *Douglas v Hello!* (2001)) and the scope of the right to privacy may be reduced where:

(i) Part of a claimant's right to privacy is sold in a commercial transaction (as in *Douglas v Hello!* (2001));

(ii) Personal information arising from a transient personal relationship will be afforded less protection than information arising out of marriage and other stable relationships (*Garry Flitcroft v Mirror Group Newspapers Ltd (A v B & Another)* (2002)); and

(iii) Arguably (*Naomi Campbell v Mirror Group Newspapers* (2004) and *Garry Flitcroft v Mirror Group Newspapers Ltd (A v B & Another)* (2002)), the protection afforded by privacy may also be reduced where the claimant is a public figure and he/she chooses to present a false image of themselves and make untrue pronouncements about their lives.

(b) Clearly, the right to privacy must be balanced against the right of freedom of expression both in:

(i) Determining whether there is an actionable breach of confidence (*e.g. Naomi Campbell v Mirror Group Newspapers* (2004)); and

(ii) The availability of interim relief (*Garry Flitcroft v Mirror Group Newspapers Ltd (A v B & Another)* (2002)). This is unsurprising, given HRA 1998, s.12(3). The relevant test for interim relief is summarised in Chapter 2, above. *Obiter* comments in the *Flitcroft* decision placed great emphasis on the freedom of the Press; it is not enough for the claimant merely to demonstrate that there is no public interest in publication—he/she must demonstrate that any interference in the freedom of the Press must be justified. The weaker the claim to privacy or the greater the public interest in publication, the more likely it is that an interim injunction to restrain publication will not be granted.

It should be noted that photographs seem to be treated differently to other media here. There appears to be a developing strand of case law (both from the UK courts, *e.g. Naomi Campbell v Mirror Group Newspapers* (2004) and the European Court of Human Rights, *e.g. Von Hannover v Germany* (2004)), that publication of the visual portrayal of private information (*i.e.* photographs or CCTV stills) is more likely to be prevented than the equivalent verbal portrayal (*i.e.* a written account of the same activity), particularly where the publication concerned is part of the tabloid press. In the *Von Hannover* decision it was noted that "... the decisive factor in balancing the protection of private life against freedom of expression should lie in the contribution that the published photographs ... [made] ... to a debate of general interest".

(c) It is unclear as to how far the UK courts will follow the jurisprudence of the European Court of Human Rights. Although the House of Lords has indicated that UK courts already tend to follow the European Court of Human Rights' approach to Art.10 and that UK courts "would often be aided" by a similar approach to Art.8, the UK courts sometimes follow the jurisprudence of the European Court of Human Rights and they sometimes ignore it. For example:

  (i) While the Human Rights Act 1998 is stated only to apply to public authorities, the UK courts do recognise (*e.g.* see *Naomi Campbell v Mirror Group Newspapers* (2004)) that Art.8 and Art.10 also apply to disputes between private individuals and between private individuals and non-government bodies. Here, therefore, UK law is consistent with the jurisprudence of the European Court of Human Rights; however

  (ii) Will the UK courts address implications of the European Court of Human Rights' decision in *Peck v UK* (2003)? In *Peck* it was held that English law failed to provide the applicant with an adequate remedy following the breach of his right to privacy. This question is, therefore, a significant one; the *Peck* decision is a strong indication that the action of breach of confidence does not provide an adequate remedy to the right to privacy in this jurisdiction.

Elements of the action for breach of confidence

The key case in breach of confidence is *Coco v Clarke* (1969), in which Mr Justice Megarry established the essential elements for a successful action in breach of confidence. Here, the claimant had disclosed details as to the design and proposals for manufacture of a moped engine. After some disagreements, the defendants proceeded to manufacture their own engine and the claimant applied for an interim injunction to restrain the defendants using information that he had disclosed. The claimant failed. To succeed, the relevant information must have the necessary quality of confidence, the information must be communicated in circumstances importing an obligation of confidence, and there must be unauthorised use of the information (the claimant only satisfied the second element of this test).

ELEMENTS OF THE ACTION OF BREACH OF CONFIDENCE: THE NECESSARY QUALITY OF CONFIDENCE

Introduction

The information may take any form; a verbal disclosure, in writing, via a drawing etc. Etchings were held to have the necessary quality of confidence in *Prince Albert v Strange* (1849), as was the genetic information contained in nectarine budwood in an Australian case (*Franklin v Giddins* (1978)).

The mere fact that the information is encrypted seems to be insufficient on its own to succeed in an action for breach of confidence (the other two elements of the action must still be satisfied, *Mars UK Ltd v Teknowledge Ltd* (2000)).

Types of information

There are no limitations to the type of information that can be protected by the law of confidence. The action can be used for commercial secrets, government secrets and to protect personal secrets:

(a) Commercial secrets. *E.g. Seager v Copydex (No.1)* (1967) concerned commercial information.
(b) Government secrets. *E.g. A-G v Guardian Newspapers (No2) "Spycatcher"* (1990) concerned government information.
(c) Personal secrets. *E.g. Argyll v Argyll* (1967) concerned personal secrets.

There are two exceptions to the general principle that any type of information can be protected by the action of breach of confidence:

(i) The courts will not protect "trivial tittle tattle" (*Coco v Clarke* (1969)). What constitutes trivial information is unclear, but this must be a very narrow category as the courts have afforded protection to information without any apparent commercial value;

(ii) Immorality. The courts should not act as censors or arbiters of taste (*Garry Flitcroft v Mirror Group Newspapers Ltd (A v B & Another)* (2002)).

"The necessary quality of confidence"

For information to have the necessary quality of confidence, it must not be public property or knowledge (*Saltman Engineering v Campbell Engineering* (1948)). So, once the information is in the public domain, it cannot generally be regarded as being confidential. Yet, information need not be absolutely confidential in order to have the necessary quality of confidence; relative secrecy may suffice, as confidentiality is a matter of degree (*Franchi v Franchi* (1967)). The information must be clearly identifiable, and be sufficiently well developed so as to be capable of realisation (*De Maudsley v Palumbo* (1996)).

ELEMENTS OF THE ACTION FOR BREACH OF CONFIDENCE: THE OBLIGATION OF CONFIDENCE

There must be an obligation of confidence arising from the circumstances in which the information was imparted (*Coco v A.N. Clark (Engineering) Ltd* (1969)). The obligation need not be express, as the courts have been prepared to imply an obligation of confidence in certain circumstances (*e.g.* in *Ackroyds v Islington Plastics* (1962), the court held that there had been a breach of an implied contractual term and a duty of confidence to use the information, in the shape of the tool, only for the purposes for which it was supplied.)

Circumstances giving rise to an obligation of confidence

Each of the circumstances that could give rise to an obligation of confidence shall be examined in turn:

(a) From contract. Where there is express contractual provisions as to confidentiality, the terms of the contract will dictate as to whether an obligation is imposed. Where, as in *Fraser v Evans* (1969), there is no express reciprocal duty, none will be implied.

(b) From an existing relationship. An obligation might arise from:

    (i) Commercial Relationships. In pre-existing commercial relationships, an obligation may be implied. Traditionally, this has been regarded as an objective question, *i.e.* on the basis of the understanding of the reasonable man (*Coco v A.N. Clark (Engineering) Ltd* (1969)). This is probably the preferred approach, despite Mr Justice Jacob's assertion in *Carflow Products v Linwood Securities* (1996), that the equitable nature of the law of confidence suggests a subjective approach.

    (ii) Employment relationships. Here, duties of confidence are particularly significant and, due to the differing interests of ex-employees and their former employers, a major distinction is drawn between the extent of the obligation implied for current as opposed to former employees.

    The main case in this area is *Faccenda Chickens v Fowler* (1987). Here it was said that where there is or was a contract of employment, the contract determines the extent of employee's obligations. If there are no express terms, then implied terms including the duty of good faith or fidelity will be imposed on the employee. *Hivac Ltd v Park Royal Scientific Instruments Ltd* (1946) provides that the duty of fidelity involves not only the protection of commercial secrets, but also a duty not to compete with the employer (legitimate preparation to compete is permitted).

    The ex-employee is less restricted. The implied term only extends to protecting information so highly confidential so it would amount to a trade secret (*Faccenda Chickens v Fowler* (1987)).

(c) Professional relationships. Professional advisors owe an obligation to those that they advise.

(d) Statute. Relevant statutory provisions include the Official Secrets Act 1989 and CDPA 1988, s.85.

Status of the third party recipient of confidential information

As a general rule, a third party who is in possession of information which he *knows* is confidential, is subject to an obligation of confidence (*Prince Albert* (1849)). There is some debate as to what constitutes sufficient knowledge for the conscience of the third party to be bound, but the innocent recipient is clearly not bound by an obligation of confidence (*Valeo Vision v Flexible Lamps* (1995)).

ELEMENTS OF THE ACTION FOR BREACH OF CONFIDENCE: UNAUTHORISED USE

This is the third element of the *Coco* (1969) test. There must be actual or threatened use of the confidential information, in breach of the obligation of confidence.

Intent is irrelevant, as to unauthorised use an objective approach (*Sir Elton John & Ors v Countess Joulebine* (2001)) is taken and there is no need for the breach to be deliberate or unconscious. In *Seager* (1967), the claimant was in breach of his obligation of confidence, despite acting honestly. So-called subconscious use also constitutes use (as per *Seager* (1967)).

DEFENCES

(i) Lapse of time (breach of confidence is an equitable action, see *Peter Pan Manufacturing Corp v Corsets Silhouette Ltd* (1964)).

(ii) Information is in the public domain. Here the information is no longer confidential. An example is *Mustad v Dosen* (1968), where the claimant disclosed previously secret information by publishing them in a patent application.

(iii) The public interest defence. Traditionally, a very narrow definition of public interest was adopted (*e.g. Initial Services v Putterill* (1967)), but in *Lion Laboratories v Evans* (1985), a more general public interest in the preservation of confidences was be outweighed by a countervailing public interest in favour of disclosure. The courts have always recognised that there is a wide difference between what is interesting to the public and what is in the public interest to make known. This distinction appears to have been blurred by Lord Woolf in *Flitcroft*, who seemed to depart from the usual public interest test in holding that the test should be what the public *want to know* and what they have a *legitimate interest* to know, rather than what they *need to know*.

REMEDIES

Remedies are discussed in general in Chapter 2. The following remedies are available to an action for breach of confidence:

  (i) Injunctions.
 (ii) Damages (*e.g. Seager v Copydex (No.1)* (1967)).
 (iv) Account of profits. *E.g. Peter Pan Manufacturing Corp v Corsets Silhouette Ltd* (1964).
  (v) Delivery up, modification or destruction upon oath.

In addition, there is the *springboard doctrine*. If confidential information is put in the public domain, the person who owed the duty may be prevented from using that information for a period of time; he cannot use his breach of confidence as a "springboard" to launch his own project. *E.g. Terrapin Ltd v Builders Supply Co (Hayes) Ltd* (1967).

5. TRADE MARK LAW

INTRODUCTION

Function of trade marks

The function of an ordinary trade mark is to act as an indicator of trade origin, this aids both consumers of branded goods and the trade mark proprietor as follows:

  (i) The trade mark acts as an indicator of quality and reliability, protecting consumers from confusion or deception in the marketplace.
 (ii) The trade mark can be enforced to protect the mark's proprietor against certain acts of unfair competition.

UK and EU trade mark law

UK trade marks are governed by the provisions of the Trade Marks Act 1994 (TMA 1994), which implements the Trade Marks directive (European Council Directive No.89/104/EEC). An

application for a national trade mark may be made to the Trade
Mark Registry (part of the UK Patent Office). It is also possible to
apply for Community trade marks (CTMs)—trade marks that are
valid in the entire EU. These are governed by the Community
Trade Mark regulation (Council Regulation (EC) No 40/94) and
applications for CTMs are considered by the CTM Office—
known as the Office for Harmonisation in the Internal Market
(Trade Marks and Designs) (OHIM).

Although most IP law courses focus on UK law, and therefore
the provisions of the TMA 1994, students will quickly realise the
great influence that ECJ jurisprudence has on UK trade mark law
and they will therefore have also to be aware of the provisions of
both the directive and the regulation because:

- Where national courts make preliminary rulings by the
  ECJ on trade mark matters, the ECJ will refer to the
  directive; and

- The ECJ is also the final arbiter on CTM matters, and here
  the regulation will be referred to.

Many of the registrability provisions in the UK TMA 1994 are
mirrored in the directive and the regulation. With this in mind,
the student might find the following table, which contains the
main UK trade mark registrability criteria that are discussed in
this book, together with the equivalent provisions in the regulation and the directive, helpful:

**The absolute and relative grounds for refusal in the Trade
Marks Act 1994, the Trade Mark Regulation (EC) No 40/94
and the Trade Mark Directive 89/104/EEC**

	UK Trade Mark Act 1994	Trade Mark Regulation	Trade Mark Directive
Definition of a trade mark	s.1(1)	Art.4	Art.2
Absolute grounds for refusal			
Signs not meeting the definition of a trade mark	s.3(1)(a)	Art.7(1)(a)	Art.3(1)(a)
Marks devoid of distinctive character	s.3(1)(b)	Art.7(1)(b)	Art.3(1)(b)

Signs that are exclusively descriptive	s.3(1)(c)	Art.7(1)(c)	Art.3(1)(c)
Signs that are exclusively generic	s.3(1)(d)	Art.7(1)(d)	Art.3(1)(d)
Inherent shapes	s.3(2)(a)	Art.7(1)(e)(i)	Art.3(1)(e)
Functional shapes	s.3(2)(b)	Art.7(1)(e)(ii)	Art.3(1)(e)
Valuable shapes	s.3(2)(c)	Art.7(1)(e)(iii)	Art.3(1)(e)
Marks contrary to morality or public policy	s.3(3)(a)	Art.7(1)(f)	Art.3(1)(f)
Marks likely to deceive the public	s.3(3)(b)	Art.7(1)(g)	Art.3(1)(g)
Marks prohibited by UK or EU law	s.3(4)	—	Art.3(2)(a)
Specially protected emblems	s.4	Art.7(1)(i)	Art.3(2)(c)
Applications made in bad faith	s.3(6)	—	Art.3(2)(d)
Relative grounds for refusal			
Conflict with an earlier identical mark for identical goods or services	s.5(1)	Art.8(1)(a)	Art.4(1)(a)
Conflict with an earlier identical mark for similar goods or services	s.5(2)(a)	Art.8(1)(b)	Art.4(1)(b)
Conflict with a similar earlier mark for identical or similar goods or services	s.5(2)(b)	Art.8(1)(b)	Art.4(1)(b)
Conflict with a mark of repute	s.5(3)	Art.8(2)(c)	Art.4(2)(d)
Conflict with earlier rights	s.5(4)	Art.8(4)	Art.4(4)(b) and 4(4)(c)

Collective marks and certification marks

Although rare, such trade marks perform different functions as compared to ordinary trade marks.

Certification marks (TMA 1994, s.50) are intended to indicate that goods or services comply with a certain objective standards as to quality, origin, material, the mode of manufacture of goods

or the performance of services or other characteristics. Any third
party whose goods or services meet the requisite standards may
apply to be an authorised user of a certification mark and the
proprietor cannot refuse this request.

Collective marks serve to indicate members of an association.
A third party who is not a member of that association does not
have the right to use the mark. Collective marks can act as certification marks and vice versa.

Trade mark law

Not all marks are capable of being registered as trade marks.
Objections to the registration of a mark may be raised, either by
the Trade Marks Registry during examination or by third parties
during opposition proceedings. The grounds for refusing registration are divided into two categories:

(a) *Absolute grounds* for refusal (TMA 1994, ss.3 and 4), which
    are concerned with objections based on the mark itself.
(b) *Relative grounds* for refusal (TMA 1994, s.5), these are
    concerned with a conflict with third party rights.

Classification of marks

The Nice Agreement for the International Classification of Goods
and Services provides that there are 34 classes of goods and eight
classes of services. Any application for registration must stipu-
late which classes, or sub-classes, in which registration is sought.
Multi-class applications are possible and it would be possible to
register a mark in respect of all 42 classes, but this is unlikely as
applicants must have a bona fide intent to use the mark for the
proscribed goods and services (TMA 1994, ss.3(6) and 32(3)).

Limited registration for retail service marks, long thought
unregistrable in the UK, is now possible in Class 35. This change
in UK practice follows OHIM's decision in *Giacomelli Sports Spa*
(1999).

Definition of a trade mark—introduction

TMA 1994, s.1(1) provides that a trade mark is a *sign* capable of
being *represented graphically*, capable of *distinguishing* goods or
services of one undertaking from those of another undertaking.

Each of the elements of this definition shall now be considered in turn.

Definition of a trade mark—a "sign"

The concept of a "sign" in UK trade mark law is very broad. Although there is no definition provided in the Act, a non-exhaustive list of examples is: words, designs, letters, numerals or the shape of goods or their packaging (TMA 1994, s.1(1)). A sign could be regarded as being *anything that conveys information* (*Phillips v Remington* (1998)). For pragmatic reasons, it can be helpful to consider signs as falling into two categories:

(a) Conventional trade marks, *i.e.* pictoral marks such as letters, words and pictures or drawings; and
(b) Non-conventional trade marks, *e.g.*:
   (i) slogans;
   (ii) three-dimensional signs (shapes);
   (iii) colours;
   (iv) sensory signs, *e.g.* auditory (sound) signs, gustatory (taste) signs and olfactory (scent) signs;
   (v) action signs; and
   (vi) holograms.

Generally speaking, it is easier to register so-called conventional marks—unconventional marks are more difficult to register. In general this is due to one or more of the following: difficulties in graphic representation, lack of distinctiveness and/or the TMA 1994, s.3(2) restrictions on registering shape marks.

Definition of a trade mark—"graphic representation"

Signs must be represented graphically, *i.e.* they must be represented in such a way that third parties may determine and understand what the sign is. In *Ralf Seickmann* (2002), the ECJ set out the test for graphic representation: graphic representations use images, lines and characters and they must be:

(i) Clear;
(ii) Precise;
(iii) Self-contained;
(iv) Easily accessible and intelligible (in the sense that it does not require the public to undertake excessive effort to

understand it, according to the Advocate-General in *Libertel Groep BV v Benelux Markenbureau* (2004));

(v) Durable; and

(vi) Objective.

Clearly, including an image of signs that comprise of slogans or words would be sufficient to graphically represent such marks. However, it can be difficult to graphically represent unconventional marks, and it is instructive here to consider the relevant case law and Trade Mark Registry guidance, for example:

(i) Three-dimensional signs are best graphically represented by photographs or line drawings of the shape from a number of different perspectives. A verbal description of the shape alone is insufficient (*Swizzels Matlow Ltd's Application* (1998));

(ii) Colours—it is specific *shades* of a colour that can be registered, either in the form of a single colour or as colour combinations. While trade mark applications commonly include a specimen of the relevant colour, *Libertel* (2003) confirms that colour specimens are not sufficiently durable to satisfy the *Seickmann* criteria; graphic representation of colour therefore now requires the designation of the relevant colour(s) using an internationally recognised colour identification system (the PANTONE system is the one most commonly used). In *Heidelberger* (2004), the ECJ specified that, in addition, colour combinations had to be represented in a systematic way;

(iii) Auditory signs are best graphically represented by musical notation (*Shield Mark BV v Kist* (2003)), although it was conceded in the *Shield Mark* decision that a written description of an auditory mark could suffice (in most cases, however, this will lack the precision and clarity demanded by the *Seickmann* criteria). In *Shield Mark*, the use of onomatopoeia to represent an animal sound was deemed to be insufficient and the ECJ did not provide guidance as to whether sonograms or digital recordings could be used to graphically represent sounds;

(iv) Gustatory signs are unlikely to succeed in trade mark registration following OHIM's decision in *Eli Lilly & Co's Community Trade Mark Application* (2003), where *Seickmann* was applied to hold that a verbal description was insufficient for a taste (here, an artificial strawberry flavour) to be graphically represented. As it is difficult to envisage another means of graphically representing tastes that would satisfy the *Seickmann* criteria, this means that it is highly unlikely that gustatory signs will be registrable as trade marks;

(v) Olfactory signs now seem to encounter similar difficulties. Although pre-*Seickmann* some scents had been registered as trade marks (the written description of scents had previously been deemed sufficient for graphic representation in relation to *Vennootshap onder Firma Scenta Aromatic Marketing's Application (THE SCENT OF FRESHLY-CUT GRASS)* (1999) and this was followed, for example, in *Myles Ltd's Community Trade Mark Application (THE SCENT OF RASPBERRIES)* (2002)), a more restrictive approach is now taken. In *Seickmann*, verbal description, chemical formula and a sample were all rejected as being insufficient to graphically represent a scent. As it is difficult to envisage another means of graphically representing tastes that would satisfy the *Seickmann* criteria, this means that it is highly unlikely that olfactory signs will be registrable as trade marks;

(vi) Action signs are, in effect, animated pictoral or word marks, *e.g.* a rotating Earth globe. They are often used on Internet web sites and although there is no clear UK authority as to the graphical representation of such marks, it would be reasonable to assume that the provision of a sequence of "still" images that represented the essential features of the action sign would be sufficient; and

(vii) Holograms *per se* are not capable of graphic representation (*Checkpoint Security Services Limited's Application* (1999)), but where the multiple features of a hologram can be *accurately* represented in still images (this would require various pictorial views showing the essential features of the hologram as it is observed from different angles), then this may be sufficient.

Definition of a trade mark—capable of distinguishing

Signs must be capable of distinguishing goods or services of one undertaking from those of another undertaking. Any sign that has the capacity to distinguish will satisfy this limited requirement (*AD2000 Trade Mark* (1996)).

ABSOLUTE GROUNDS FOR REFUSAL

Introduction

A sign will not be registered if it falls within one or more of the absolute grounds for refusing registration. Each absolute ground is considered below.

Signs not satisfying the s.1(1) requirements

Signs which do not meet the definition of "trade mark" provided in the TMA 1994 shall not be registered (TMA 1994, s.3(1)(a)), *i.e.* where the mark is not properly represented on the application form or is incapable of distinguishing, the application will fail.

The basic elements of *graphic representation* have already been considered above. It is important for a trade mark applicant not to make a mistake as to graphic representation, as the opportunity to correct such mistakes are limited (TMA 1994, s.39 prevents the correction of errors in a trade mark application that would substantially affect the identity of the trade mark). This is mitigated by the fact that it is UK Registry practice (in response to the decision in *TY-NANT* (1999)) to examine marks for graphic representation before a filing date is allocated.

Signs must also be *capable of distinguishing* the goods or services of one undertaking from those of other undertakings. As noted above, this is not a high standard and, in effect, it will only bar those signs that are incapable of functioning as trade marks (*e.g.* the Philips shaver shape in *Philips Electronics v Remington Consumer Products* (1999), a case discussed in relation to shape marks below, was held not to be distinctive in a trade mark sense and thus did not satisfy TMA 1994, s.3(1)(a)).

Proviso to TMA 1994, s.3(1)(b)(c) and (d)

Marks devoid of distinctive character or those consisting of exclusively descriptive or generic signs are prohibited *unless it can be shown that before the application was made, the mark has acquired a distinctive character as a result of the use made of it* (TMA 1994, s.3(1)). This proviso to TMA 1994, ss.3(1)(b),(c) and (d) means that there is no absolute prohibition as a matter of law on non-distinctive, descriptive and generic marks. As recognised in *British Sugar v James Robertson (TREAT)* (1996), such marks may be registered where they have become factually distinctive upon use despite the prohibitions stated in TMA 1994 s.3(1)(b)–(d).

This proviso is generally thought *not* to apply to TMA 1994, s.3(1)(a) and certainly does not apply to any other absolute ground for refusal.

Marks devoid of distinctive character

TMA 1994, s.3(1)(b) prevents the registration of marks that are not *prima facie* distinctive. In *British Sugar v James Robertson (TREAT)* (1996)), it was said that a mark is devoid of distinctive character where the sign cannot distinguish the applicant's goods or services without the public first being educated that it is a trade mark. Therefore, trade marks will only fail under TMA 1994, s.3(1)(b) where they are not distinctive by nature and have not become distinctive by nurture (*AD2000 Trade Mark* (1996)). The UK Trade Mark Registry considers that signs consisting of two numbers or numerals and signs prohibited from registration under TMA 1994, ss.3(1)(c) or (d) combined with any other non-distinctive matter, to be non-distinctive (of course the proviso makes it possible for such a mark to *acquire* distinctiveness, after which it may be registerable). Nevertheless, there may be some conflict here with the ECJ's view that where a sign consists of a *combination* of letters and numbers (an example of a so-called compound mark), that the sign should be viewed as a whole; according to the ECJ it is not correct to consider the distinctiveness of each element of the compound mark separately (*Sat.1 Satellitenfernsehen GmbH v OHIM (SAT.1)* (2004)).

Although in practice trade mark applications for unconventional marks (and certain conventional word marks, namely common surnames and slogans) often fail under TMA 1994, s.3(1)(b), the same legal standard of distinctiveness applies to all marks. This point has been directly addressed by the ECJ in a relation to common surnames and shape marks (in *Nichols plc v Registrar of Trade Marks* (2004) and *Mag Instrument Inc v OHIM* (2004) respectively). That being said, it should be noted that the ECJ does make some practical distinctions in recognising that the relevant public's perception of certain marks (*e.g.* colours, shapes and slogans) is not necessarily the same as for other types of marks and that only where such marks depart significantly from the norm or customs of the sector, and which therefore fulfil the essential function of indicating origin, will such marks not be devoid of distinctive character (*e.g.* see *Libertel* and also *Mag Instrument Inc v OHIM* (2004)).

Finally, in *Koninklijke KPN Nederland v Benelux-Merkenbureau (POSTKANTOOR)* (2002), the ECJ noted that a word mark which is descriptive (see the discussion of TMA 1994, s.3(1)(c), below) is inherently devoid of distinctiveness. Although it should be emphasised that each of the absolute grounds for refusal are, in law, independent of the others and should be examined separately, the *POSTKANTOOR* decision means that, in fact, word marks that fail under TMA 1994, s.3(1)(c) will also be bad for s.3(1)(b).

Signs that are exclusively descriptive

For a sign to be open to objection under TMA 1994, s.3(1)(c), the trade mark must consist *exclusively* of a sign which may be used in trade to describe characteristics of the goods or services.

The sub-categories of TMA 1994, s.3(1)(c) are:

(i) Kind. Terms indicating kind or type that should be free for all traders to use, *e.g.* PERSONAL for computers, are not normally registrable.

(ii) Quality. Laudatory words, *e.g.* PERFECTION, are not usually registrable.

(iii) Quantity. The Trade Mark Registry gives the example that 454 would not be registrable for butter, as butter is frequently sold for domestic consumption in 454g (1lb) packs. Where numerical marks are not descriptive or otherwise objectionable, they may be registered.

(iv) Intended purpose. Generally, words referring to the purpose of goods or services are not registrable.

(v) Value. Signs pertaining to the value of goods or services are not normally registrable, *e.g.* BUY ONE, GET ONE FREE.

(vi) Geographical origin. Geographical names are not usually registrable unless used in specific circumstances. A fanciful use of a geographic name, *e.g.* EQUATOR for ice, would be permissible as here the name is unlikely to be taken as the origin of the goods.

(vii) Time of production of goods or the rendering of services. Typically, marks such as SAME DAY DELIVERY for courier services or AUTUMN 2005 for haute couture would not be registrable.

(viii) Other characteristics of goods or services. For example, a representations of the good or service would not be usually registrable.

Marks falling into any of these categories may still be registrable if they have become distinctive upon use (the TMA 1994, s.3(1) proviso). There has been a considerable degree of confusion as to what constitutes a descriptive mark, with conflicting guidance emanating from the ECJ in a variety of decisions; *Windsurfing Chiemsee v Attenberger* (1999), *Proctor & Gamble v OHIM (BABY DRY)* (2002) and *OHIM v Wrigley (DOUBLEMINT)* (2003) are the most important of these.

The *Windsurfing Chiemsee* decision, which concerned the geographical name CHIEMSEE, indicated that it was in the public interest that a restrictive approach should be taken to the registration of descriptive marks in general. In relation to geographic names, in particular, the test should be: is the geographic name, or would it be in the future, capable in the mind of the relevant consumer of designating the trade origin of the goods in question? Although the subsequent *BABY DRY* decision, which concerned the use of BABY DRY for nappies, did not address the issue of geographic names, it signalled that a wider category of descriptive marks may be registrable; where the consumer viewing the mark would see it as being a trade mark, and not a descriptive or entirely generic indication, then it should be acceptable for registration. It seems that any perceptible difference between a descriptive term, as normally used, and the trade mark application at issue would be sufficient to satisfy the criterion of distinctiveness—in this particular decision, the difference was the syntaxically unusual juxtaposition of BABY and DRY that was not a familiar expression in English and was not the normal way of describing nappies (*i.e.* the inversion of "dry baby" to "baby dry" created sufficient difference to escape TMA 1994, s.3(1)(c)). Finally, the ECJ in the *DOUBLEMINT* decision, which concerned the use of DOUBLEMINT for mint chewing gum, seems, in practice, to have retrenched from the liberal *BABY DRY* approach to descriptive marks in saying that a mark must be refused registration if at least one of its possible meanings designates a characteristic of the goods or services concerned. Thus the ECJ seems to be advocating a more restrictive general approach to descriptive marks.

What the current test is for a descriptive mark is, therefore, unclear. In the view of this author, *Chiemsee* (1999) remains a d authority for geographical names and for descriptive .arks in general, after noting the confusion over the correct test for descriptive marks, the current test may well be "if at least one of the possible meanings of a mark designates a characteristic of the goods or services concerned, then it fails for TMA 1994, s.3(1)(c) (*DOUBLEMINT* (2003)), <u>but</u> where a mark has descriptive elements that are combined to form an unusual variation (*BABY DRY* (2002), but given *Chiemsee* (1999) and *DOUBLEMINT* (2003), the standard for this is likely to be higher than indicated in *BABY DRY* itself), then this may be sufficient for the mark to satisfy TMA 1994, s.3(1)(c)".

Signs that are exclusively generic

TMA 1994, s.3(1)(d) prohibits the registration of signs or indications that have become customary in the current language or in the bona fide and established practices of the trade. An example can be found in *JERYL LYNN Trade Mark* (1999), where an application for JERYL LYNN for vaccines was refused as the mark described a strain of vaccine and was not distinctive of the applicant. Similarly, in *RFU v Cotton Traders* (2002) a pictoral mark (an image of a red rose) was rejected as it was not distinctive of the applicant.

There is also some ECJ guidance in this area. *Mertz v Krell (BRAVO)* (2001) clarifies that a restrictive approach should be take to this provision; TMA 1994, s.3(1)(d) should be interpreted as only precluding registration of a trade mark where the signs or indications of which the mark was exclusively composed had become customary in the current language or in the bona fide and established practices of the trade to designate the <u>same</u> goods or services for which registration of that mark was sought.

As with TMA 1994, ss.3(1)(b) and (c), objections under this absolute ground for refusal may be overcome by the proviso, as in *Waterford Wedgewood v David Nagli Ltd* (1998), where the registration of LISMORE was challenged. The defendant argued that LISMORE was the name of a pattern and style of cut glass and therefore the application should be barred under TMA 1994, s.3(1)(d). As the TMA 1994, s.3(1) proviso applied (there was evidence that the name had become distinctive of the applicant's glass), registration was allowed.

Unregisterable shapes

Traditionally in the UK, shapes were not registerable (see *Coca-Cola's Trade Mark Applications* (1986)). The TMA 1994 makes it clear that the shapes of goods and their packaging are now registerable (TMA 1994, s.1(1)), but TMA 1994, s.3(2) does exclude certain shapes from registration.

Although it is accepted that shapes can be registered as trade marks provided they satisfy the normal tests for registrability, in <u>practice</u>, difficulties with shape marks are often encountered with TMA 1994, ss.3(1)(b) (*e.g.* see *Société de Produits Nestlé SA v Unilever plc (VIENNETTA)* (2002)) as well as 3(2).

The leading authority on shape marks is *Koninklijike Philips Electronics NV v Remington Consumer Products* (2002), known as the *Philips* razor case. Phillips had long produced and sold a three-headed rotary shaver (the Philishave). When Remington introduced a rotary shaver of similar design (the DT55), Philips sued for infringement of a mark which constituted the face of the three-headed shaver, and the UK Court of Appeal (*Philips Electronics v Remington Consumer Products* (1999)) referred a number of issues relating to shape marks to the ECJ. The guidance provided by the ECJ in *Koninklijike Philips Electronics NV v Remington Consumer Products* (2002) in relation to TMA 1994, s.3(2) is set out below, together with other relevant cases:

(a) Where the shape results from the nature of the goods themselves they cannot be registered (TMA 1994, s.3(2)(a)). This is a bar to what could be termed *inherent shapes* such as the shape of an umbrella. In *Philips* (2002) this issue was not directly addressed by the ECJ, but as electric shavers could take other forms, there would be no objection to Philips' three-headed razor shape on this ground. The approach to TMA 1994, s.3(2)(a) is still not certain, as illustrated in *Société de Produits Nestlé SA v Unilever plc (VIENNETTA)* (2002), which concerned the shape of the Viennetta ice cream dessert, where it was noted that it was unclear as to whether "the nature of the goods" should be given a narrow interpretation (*i.e.* the actual item for which registration is sought, here the Viennetta ice cream) or a wide interpretation (the *type* of goods for which registration is sought, here, ice cream desserts). ECJ guidance will have to be sought on this point, but it is the view of this author that *Linde AG (&*

        others) v Deutsches Patent-und Markenant Cases (2002) can be read to indicate that the ECJ would tend to favour the wide interpretation.

(b) Where the shape of the goods is necessary to achieve a technical result (TMA 1994, s.3(2)(b)). This is a bar to what could be termed *functional shapes* such as the head of a screwdriver. *Philips* (2002) indicates that "necessary" should not be interpreted too narrowly, the purpose of this provision is to prevent the registration of shapes whose essential characteristics perform a technical function, with the result that the exclusivity in the trade mark right would impose restrictions or limitations on third parties producing competing products. Therefore (i) where essential characteristics of a shape are functional, the application will fail under TMA 1994, s.3(2)(b), and (ii) even where other shapes could achieve the same technical result as the shape sought to be protected as a trade mark, this will not overcome an objection under TMA 1994, s.3(2)(b). An earlier UK decision, *Proctor & Gamble Co's Trade Mark Application* (1998), took a similar approach. It is clear, therefore, that where shapes have significant function elements, they will fail under TMA 1994, s.3(2)(b).

(c) Where the shape gives substantial value to the goods (TMA 1994, s.3(2)(c)). This is a bar to what could be termed *valuable shapes*, such as a porcelain container for gin in the shape of a traditional Dutch house (rather than the usual glass bottle). There is no ECJ guidance here, but in *Phillips* (1999), the Court of Appeal upheld Mr Justice Jacob's earlier findings in *Philips Electronics v Remington Consumer Products* (1998) that a valuable shape in this context can be identified where the shape itself adds substantial value, *e.g.* the shape adds value via eye appeal or functional effectiveness. In contrast, shapes that are valuable because they are "good trade marks" would not fall foul of TMA 1994, s.3(2)(c). Despite that, the UK Trade Mark Registry arguably takes too stringent an approach to this section (see *e.g. Dualit Ltd's Trade Mark Applications* (1999)) and clarification is needed here.

Marks likely to offend morals or deceive

A mark shall not be registered if it is contrary to public policy or accepted principles of morality (TMA 1994, s.3(3)(a)) or is of such a nature that it is likely to deceive the public (TMA 1994, s.3(3)(b)), for example as to the nature, quality or origin of the goods or services.

Relatively few marks are likely to be deemed contrary to public policy or morality as only the most shocking or outrageous terms should be denied registration under TMA 1994, s.3(3)(a) (*Ghazilian's Trade Mark Application* (2001)). It is clear that marks that are in poor taste will not be caught by this provision, only where principles of morality are offended will registration be refused under TMA 1994, s.3(3)(a) (see, for example OHIM's ruling in *Dick Lexic Ltd (DICK AND FANNY)* (2003)). Morality should be considered in the context of current thinking. Only where a substantial number of persons would be offended (such persons might, nevertheless, be in a minority in the community) should registration be refused; the context in which the allegedly offensive mark is to be used may be a factor in this assessment (*Ghazilian's Trade Mark Application* (2001)). This approach was followed in *Basic Trademark SA's Application (JESUS)* (2005), where it was also noted that, under the Human Rights Act 1998, due account also had to be taken of the applicant's right of freedom of expression.

In relation to TMA 1994, s.3(3)(b), *BOCM's Application (EUROLAMB)* (1997) is relevant. Here, EUROLAMB was considered to be deceptive (TMA 1994, s.3(3)(b)) if used in relation to non-sheep meat (when used in relation to sheep meat, it was descriptive). It is clear that the test of deception is objective, actual evidence of deception must be provided and that mere advertising "puffs" are not deemed to be deceptive (*Kraft Jacobs Suchard Ltd's Application* (2001)).

Marks prohibited by UK or EC law

The registration of marks whose use would be illegal under UK or Community law is precluded by TMA 1994, s.3(4). This means that marks that would contravene other UK statutes (such as the Trade Descriptions Act 1968) or Community law (*e.g.* Regulation 2081/92 regarding Protected Designations of Origin (PDOs) and Protected Geographical Indications (PGIs)) cannot be registered.

Applications made in bad faith

There is no requirement that a mark need be used prior to the application for registration, but the applicant must have a bona fide intention to use the mark (TMA 1994, s.32(3)) and applications may be refused when they are made in bad faith (TMA 1994, s.3(6)). Therefore, so-called ghost applications would be caught by this section. An example of a ghost application under the old law was *Imperial Group v Phillip Morris* (1982), where the applicant had registered the ghost mark NERIT so as to prevent others from using the word MERIT. Objections to overly-wide registrations (where the applicant registers a mark for more goods or services than he intended to use the mark in) might also be made under TMA 1994, s.3(6)—this possibility was considered in *Road Tech Computer Systems Ltd v Unison Software* (1996).

More generally, dishonesty will fall into TMA 1994, s.3(6), but activities falling short of the standards of acceptable and reasonable commercial behaviour will also be caught (*Gromax Plasticulture v Don & Low (Nonwovens)* (1999)). Some deliberate action or behaviour by the applicant is, however, required (*Kraft Jacobs Suchard Ltd's Application* (2001)).

Specially protected emblems

TMA 1994, s.4 provides details of marks that are considered to fall into the category of specially protected emblems, for example marks with Royal connotations and the Olympic symbol cannot be registered (TMA 1994, s.3(5)); marks containing such emblems may not be registered in the absence of consent.

RELATIVE GROUNDS FOR REFUSAL

Introduction

The applicant must also overcome the relative grounds for refusing registration. These relate to conflict with earlier marks or earlier rights. The "earlier mark" (TMA 1994, s.6) might be a trade mark registered in the UK or under the Madrid Protocol. Alternatively it might be a CTM or a well-known mark (the latter are entitled to protection as per Art.6*bis* of the Paris Convention for the Protection of Industrial Property 1883).

There is a defence of honest concurrent use in the TMA 1994 (TMA 1994, s.7—see below). This provision can be very useful in trade mark infringement (see below), but in relation to the relative grounds for refusal this concept is of less relevance; it has been made clear that a trade mark application must be refused, irrespective of honest concurrent use, if the registered proprietor objects (*Road Tech Computer Systems v Unison Software (ROAD-RUNNER)* (1997)). If the proprietor of the registered mark objects, honest concurrent use provides no defence and the Registry will apply the relevant sub-section of s.5.

It should be emphasised that any objections under the relative grounds for refusal can be overcome by obtaining the consent of the proprietor of the earlier mark (TMA 1994, s.5(5)).

Each relative ground for refusal is considered below.

Conflict with an earlier identical mark for identical goods or services

TMA 1994, s.5(1) provides the narrowest relative ground for refusing registration, a mark identical to an earlier trade mark and used for identical goods and services will not be registered.

The ECJ has provided some guidance in this area in *LTJ Diffusion v Sadas (ARTHUR ET FÉLICE)* (2003)—"identity" must be interpreted strictly and for a sign to be identical to any earlier trade mark it must (i) reproduce the earlier trade mark without any modification or addition, although (ii) where the sign, viewed globally from the perspective of the average consumer, contains insignificant differences to the earlier trade mark that may go unnoticed, then it will be considered to be identical to the earlier trade mark. This is a strict test for identity of marks and this means that the UK should abandon its earlier, more generous, interpretation of TMA 1994, s.5(1) (see *Decon Laboratories v Baker Scientific* (2000)).

However, the test for when goods or services are identical under TMA 1994, s.5(1) is less certain; there is no clear ECJ guidance on this, but both the ECJ (*LTJ Diffusion* (2003)) and in the UK (*British Sugar v Robinson (TREAT)* (1996)) have considered the classes for which the earlier trade mark is registered and compared these with the class(es) for which the applicant has applied for; so, it appears that comparison of trade mark classes will be a primary factor in deciding whether identity of goods and services is present.

Conflict with an earlier identical or similar mark for identical or similar goods or services

The registration of similar marks for the same or similar goods or services is only prohibited where confusion on the part of the public is likely to arise (TMA 1994, s.5(2)). Specifically, what is prohibited is the registration of:

(i) Identical marks for similar goods or services (TMA 1994, s.5(2)(a)), or

(ii) Similar marks for identical/similar goods or services (TMA 1994, s.5(2)(b)). Where, because of the identity or similarity, there is a *likelihood of confusion* on the part of the public, which includes the *likelihood of association* with the earlier trade mark.

The test for when marks are identical (TMA 1994, s.5(2)(a)) or where the goods or services are identical (TMA 1994, s.5(2)(b)) is the same as that in TMA 1994, s.5(1) (see above).

However, what constitutes "confusing similarity" has been considered at length by the ECJ (see *Sabel v Puma* (1998) and *Canon v Metro Goldwyn-Meyer (formerly Pathé)* (1999)).

What is clear is that confusion must be appreciated *globally*, taking into account *all factors relevant to the circumstances of the case*. Factors to be taken into account in this global appreciation of confusion include:

(a) The *recognition* of the earlier trade mark on the market.

(b) The *association* that can be made between the registered mark and the applicant's sign.

(c) The *degree of similarity* between <u>the mark and the sign</u> and <u>the goods or services</u>. The degree of similarity must be considered in deciding whether the similarity is sufficient so as to lead to a likelihood of confusion and this involves consideration of the following:

(i) The similarity of registered mark and the sign. Similarity of the marks in question should be judged upon consumer perception of the marks as a whole, bearing in mind their distinctive and dominant components. Similarity might be visual, phonetic or conceptual (*Sabel* (1998)), but it is accepted that consumers rarely have the opportunity to make a direct comparison of the mark and the sign and they are assumed to have an imperfect recollection (*Lloyd Schufabrik and Meyer & Co GmbH v Klijsen Handel B.V.* (2000)). The more distinctive the earlier registered mark, the greater the likelihood of confusion (*Sabel* (1998)).

(ii) The similarity of the goods or services. Goods or services might be distinguished as to, for example, their nature, end users, cost, and the normal method of purchase or methods of use. Account may be taken of the distinctive character and repute of the earlier mark in deciding whether the similarity is sufficient so as to lead to a likelihood of confusion (*Canon* (1999)).

It has also been made clear that "likelihood of association" is not an alternative to "likelihood of confusion", but serves to define its scope. This means that if the public merely makes an association between two trade marks, this would not in itself be sufficient for concluding that there is a likelihood of confusion (*Sabel* (1998)); there is no likelihood of confusion where public would not believe that goods or services came from the same undertaking.

Conflict with a mark of repute

TMA 1994, s.5(3)) provides that a mark that is identical or similar to an earlier mark will be refused registration in respect of *dissimilar* goods or services where the earlier mark is a mark of repute and the use of the later mark would, without due cause, take *unfair advantage* of or be *detrimental* to the reputed mark's distinctiveness or reputation. Following the ECJ's decision in *Davidoff v Gofkid* (2003) (followed in *Adidas-Salomon AG v Fitnessworld* (2004)), it appears that the application of TMA 1994, s.5(3) has extended beyond dissimilar goods and services and now also applies to identical or similar goods and services. Unlike TMA 1994, s.5(2), there is no requirement of confusion for this relative ground of refusal (see *Sabel* (1998), *Canon* (1999) and *Adidas-Salomon AG v Fitnessworld* (2004)).

A mark of repute is a mark with a reputation in the UK (for CTM applications, it must have a reputation in the EU). In deciding as to whether a trade mark has a reputation, the ECJ has provided some guidance (*General Motors Corp v Yplon (CHEVY)* (2000)). Repute must be judged with reference to the general public or (if appropriate to the nature of the relevant product(s) or services(s)) to a specific section of the public, and the mark must be known to a *significant portion of that public*. Relevant indicators of the public's knowledge of the mark include the extent and duration of the trade mark's use, its market share and the extent to which it has been promoted.

In order for registration to be refused under s.5(3), use of the applicant's mark will have to take unfair advantage of or be detrimental to the reputed mark's distinctiveness or reputation. On this issue of detriment, in *Oasis Stores Ltd's Application (EVEREADY)* (1998) it was said that merely being reminded of an opponent's mark did not itself amount to taking unfair advantage. The fact that the applicant did not benefit to any significant extent from the opponent's reputation and the wide divergence between the parties' goods was relevant; s.5(3) could not be intended to prevent the registration of *any mark* identical or similar to a mark of repute.

It is clear from infringement cases (the similar wording of TMA 1994 ss.5(3) and 10(3) mean that infringement cases can be relevant) that the concept of detriment is very similar to the American concept of dilution; both dilution and detriment can occur via "blurring", where the distinctiveness of a mark is eroded or by the "tarnishing" of the mark's reputation (*Premier Brands v Typhoon Europe* (2000)); nevertheless, one should be wary of describing TMA 1994, s.5(3) as an anti-dilution provision (UK lawyers and commentators are particularly guilty of this, resulting in the selective use of American dilution doctrines in the UK, which must be inimical to maintaining a European harmonised approach). It is clear, however, that the stronger a mark's distinctive character and reputation, the easier it is to establish detriment (*Premier Brands v Typhoon Europe* (2000)).

Conflict with earlier rights

TMA 1994, s.5(4) provides that where a mark conflicts with earlier rights, including passing off, copyright and design rights, the mark will not be registered.

SURRENDER, REVOCATION INVALIDITY, ACQUIESCENCE AND RECTIFICATION

(a) Surrender. It is possible to surrender one's trade mark with respect to some or all of the goods and services for which it is registered (TMA 1994, s.45).

(b) Marks may be revoked (removed from the Register) on three grounds (TMA 1994, s.45); non-use, because the mark has become generic, or because the mark has become deceptive.

(c) A mark will be invalid if it breaches any of the absolute grounds for refusing registration (TMA 1994, ss.47 and 72).

(d) Where the proprietor of an earlier trade mark or other right is aware of the use of a mark subsequently registered in the UK and has, for a continuous period of five years, taken no action regarding that use, the proprietor is said to have acquiesced. Where this is the case, the proprietor of the earlier mark or right cannot rely on his right in applying for a declaration of invalidity or in opposing the use of the later mark, unless it is being used in bad faith (TMA 1994, s.48).

(e) Any person with "a sufficient interest" can apply to rectify an error or omission in the Register. Such a rectification must not relate to matters that affect the validity of the trade mark (TMA 1994, s.64).

INFRINGEMENT

Introduction

The proprietor (and any exclusive licensee) has certain rights in his/her mark (TMA 1994, s.9(1)) which are infringed by certain forms of unauthorised use (as specified in TMA 1994, s.10) of the mark in the UK. These rights come into existence from the date of registration, which is the date of filing (TMA 1994, s.9(3)). A number of the infringement provisions are similar to the provisions that form the basis of the relative grounds for refusal (see above).

All infringing acts require the mark to be *used in the UK in the course of trade*. What constitutes sufficient use of a mark in these terms (see TMA ss.10(4) and 103(2)) has been the subject matter of some debate. *Trade* means any business or profession (TMA 1994, s.103(1)) and the ECJ has indicated that use in the course of trade occurs where the use is in the context of commercial activities with a view to gaining economic advantage (*Arsenal v Reed* (2002)). Whether use is *in the UK* can be a difficult issue. For example, *obiter* comments in *1–800 Flowers Inc v Phonenames Ltd* (2001) consider use on the Internet—merely placing a mark on the internet from a non-UK location is insufficient to constitute use in the UK; the mark proprietor must actively promote their site to members of the UK public. Lastly, there is a debate as to whether so-called non-trade mark use of a mark will infringe. This was a key issue in *Arsenal v Reed* (2002). The background to this case is important—it had been claimed that the trade mark ARSENAL that had been used on unofficial Arsenal football club merchandise by a stall holder was regarded by his consumers as being a badge of allegiance (*i.e.* the use of the mark on the unofficial merchandise indicated support of Arsenal football club) rather than as a guarantee of trade origin (*i.e.* the use of the mark on the unofficial merchandise (falsely) indicates that it comes from or is associated with Arsenal football club). Here, the ECJ indicated that non-trade mark use of a mark will infringe when such uses will or may affect the *function* of the trade mark, in particular the guarantee of trade origin function. It is unclear as to whether the ECJ considers that there are trade mark functions other than that of guarantee of origin (the House of Lords appears to have held that this is the only such function, see *R. v Johnstone* (2003)), so the scope of non-infringing non-trade mark use of a mark is still unclear.

The acts that constitute trade mark infringement are discussed below.

Use of an identical sign for identical goods or services

Use, in the course of trade, of an identical sign in respect of identical goods or services constitutes trade mark infringement (TMA 1994, s.10(1)). This form of infringement mirrors TMA 1994, s.5(1) (as confirmed in *LTJ Diffusion v Sadas* (2003)), so please refer to relative grounds for refusal, above.

Use of an identical or similar sign on identical or similar goods or services

Use, in the course of trade, of an identical sign on similar goods or services (TMA 1994, s.10(2)(a)), or a similar sign on identical or similar goods or services (TMA 1994, s.10(2)(b)) constitutes infringement where the public is likely to be confused as to the origin of the goods or services or is likely to assume that there is an association with the registered mark. This ground for infringement is the equivalent of TMA 1994, s.5(2). Please refer to the guidance provided for s.5(2), above.

Use of a mark similar to a mark of repute for dissimilar goods or services

Registered marks with a "reputation" are infringed if an identical or similar mark is used for non-similar goods or services, where the use takes unfair advantage of, or is detrimental to, the distinctive character or repute of the registered mark (TMA 1994, s.10(3)). This provision parallels that of s.5(3). Please refer to the reading and guidance provided for s.5(3), above.

Contributory infringement

TMA 1994, s.10(5) is known as the contributory infringement provision. This provision creates a form of secondary participation where a person who applies a trade mark to certain materials has actual or constructive knowledge that the use of the mark is not authorised. This provision extends infringement down the supply chain, but printers, publishers, manufacturers of packaging etc. may avoid s.10(5) liability in practice *via* the insertion of suitable standard contractual terms into their agreements with their clients.

DEFENCES TO INFRINGEMENT

There are a range of defences to trade mark infringement which are to be found in TMA 1996, ss.10(6), 11(1)–(3) and 12. As a number of these defences turn on the issue of "honest practice in industrial and commercial matters" it is appropriate to note here that the ECJ has provided some guidance to this in *Gerolsteiner Brunnen v Putsch* (2004). A defendant will have acted according to honest practice in industrial and commercial matters when they have (i) acted fairly in relation to legitimate interests of the trade mark owner and (ii) have avoided the perception that they were unfairly competing with the trade mark proprietor.

Comparative advertising

Under the Trade Mark Act 1938, comparative advertising (comparing X's goods with Y's or Y using X's mark as a way of praising his own goods) constituted infringement. Now comparative advertising is allowed (TMA 1994, ss.10(6)) under certain circumstances; in particular if the use is detrimental or takes unfair advantage of the distinctive character or repute of the trade mark, the use must be in accordance with the honest practices in industrial or commercial matters. It should be noted that there is not an equivalent provision in the trade mark Directive or Regulation to TMA 1994, s.10(6) (therefore, would the *Gerolsteiner* formulation of the test for honest practice apply?).

TMA 1994, s.10(6) itself was afforded a liberal interpretation in *British Airways PLC v Ryanair Ltd* (2001). British Airways had brought an action for trade mark infringement against Ryanair for the publication of two Ryanair advertisements comparing Ryanair fares with those of British Airways. The action failed. In assessing as to whether a mark has been used in accordance with honest practices, the court should view the advertisement as a whole. Although misleading advertisements cannot be honest based on the facts, while the advertisement at issue may have caused offence it was not dishonest and the price comparisons were not significantly unfair.

A recent interim decision, *O2 Ltd & Another v Hutchison 3G UK Ltd (BUBBLES)* (2004), emphasises the importance of the dishonesty element of the *Ryanair* comparative advertising test and also illustrates the importance that Directive (97/55/EC) on the Control of Misleading Advertising has for TMA 1994, s.10(6).

Use of another registered mark

TMA 1994, s.11(1) provides that the use of one registered mark, within the boundaries of its registration, does not infringe another registered mark.

Use of own name or address

TMA 1994, s.11(2)(a) has been interpreted to provide a defence for both natural persons (*Nichols plc v Registrar of Trade Marks* (2004)) and legal persons (*Scandecor Developments v. Scandecor Marketing* (2001), confirmed in *Reed Executive plc v Reed Business Information Ltd* (2004)) to use his/her/its own name or address, provided that the use accords with appropriate honest practices (see *Reed Executive plc v Reed Business Information Ltd* (2004)). The defence appears to be interpreted quite broadly and the *Gerolsteiner* (2004) approach (see above) to "honest practice" will apply, but it appears that mere confusion is not sufficient for a finding of dishonesty; significant actual deception is needed.

Use of certain indications

TMA 1994, s.11(2)(b) provides that the use of certain indications (*e.g.* the intended purpose of the goods or services or their geographical origin) will not constitute infringement where that use accords with appropriate honest practices. Some interesting reasoning can be found in *Allied Domceq v Murray McDavid (LAPHROAIG)* (1997), but you should have regard for the ECJ's guidance in *Gerolsteiner Brunnen GmbH v Putsch GmbH* (2004).

Use of intended purpose

TMA 1994, s.11(2)(c) provides that the use of a trade mark will not infringe where it is necessary to indicate the intended purpose of a product or service, in particular use in relation to accessories or spare parts. The ECJ has provided some guidance here in *Gillette Company, Gillette Group Finland Oy v LA- Laboratories Ltd Oy* (2005); it is clear that TMA 1994, s.11(2)(c) is not <u>limited</u> to spare parts or accessories and that a defendant will benefit from this defence where their use of a third party's trade mark was necessary (in the sense that it is the only means of providing the public with complete information on the intended purpose of the product) and that their use is honest. The concept of honesty in *Gillette* appears to be more stringent than that set out in *Gerolsteiner*. *Gillette* seems to indicate that for TMA 1994, s.11(2)(c) the following will constitute dishonest use: use that gives an impression of a commercial link between the defendant and the registered trade mark proprietor; use that affects the value of a well-known mark; and use that discredits or imitates an earlier registered trade mark.

The locality defence

According to TMA 1994, s.11(3), signs which have rights applicable to a particular locality, whose use predates the registration of a third party's trade mark may continue to be used in that locality. This provision enables a *local* user of a common law mark, *i.e.* an unregistered mark protected by passing off, to continue their use of that mark.

Exhaustion

Trade mark rights are exhausted once the proprietor has unequivocally consented to the placing of goods bearing their registered trade mark on the market within the European Economic Area (EEA) (TMA 1994, s.12(1)). The doctrine of exhaustion means that, for example, once a brand owner consents to a consignment of their goods being marketed in France, trade mark rights cannot be used to prevent that consignment of goods from being resold in the UK (unless there are legitimate reasons for this, TMA 1994, s.12(2)). Goods resold in this way are known as "grey imports" or "parallel imports". The ECJ's ruling in the joined cases of *Zino Davidoff SA v A & G Imports Ltd, Levi Strauss (UK) Ltd v Tesco Stores Ltd, Tesco plc* and *Levi Strauss (UK) Ltd and Costco Wholesale UK Ltd, formerly Costco UK Ltd* (2002) are the key authorities here.

Where, however, a trade mark proprietor has consented to the sale of goods bearing their registered trade mark *outside* the EEA, such activity cannot exhaust registered trade marks within the EEA (*i.e.* the EU does not follow the so-called "international exhaustion" doctrine).

Remedies

Remedies are discussed in general in Chapter 2. The following remedies are available for trade mark infringement:

   (i) Damages (TMA 1994, s.14(2)).
  (ii) Account of profits (TMA 1994, s.14(2)).
 (iii) Injunctions (TMA 1994, s.14(2)).
  (iv) Erasure of the offending sign (TMA 1994, s.15).
   (v) Delivery up (TMA 1994, s.16).
  (vi) Destruction or forfeiture of infringing goods (TMA 1994, s.19).

In addition:

   (i) In certain circumstances, threats to bring trade mark infringement proceedings can in themselves become actionable (TMA 1994, s.21).
  (ii) While there is no specific provision for the infringement of well-known marks that are not registered in the UK, the proprietor of such marks may restrain, by injunction, the

use of identical or similar marks used in respect of identical or similar goods where confusion would result (TMA 1994, s.56).

CRIMINAL OFFENCES

There is both general and specific provision of criminal sanctions:

(a) Trade Descriptions Act 1968 and Consumer Protection Act 1987. In practice, various offences under these Acts may be applicable to trade marks.
(b) Offences under the Trade Mark Act 1994. Unauthorised use of a trade mark may constitute an offence (see TMA 1994, s.92). Other offences include falsification of the Register (TMA 1994, s.94) and falsely representing the mark as registered (TMA 1994, s.95).

6. PASSING OFF

INTRODUCTION

Passing off is a tort, historically developed from the tort of deceit (which had proved inadequate to protect producers that were suffering due to competitor's false assertions to be related to them). Passing off protects goodwill, and as such it may be used in relation to marks, including unregistered marks (passing off is sometimes described as the law of unregistered trade marks). Many trade mark infringement cases also involve passing off issues and these two areas of law are closely related in practice.

The key criterion of a successful action in passing off is the presence of goodwill; it is goodwill, rather than the mark itself, that is protected in passing off.

PASSING OFF—WHICH TEST?

There are two possible tests for passing off:

(a) Lord Diplock identified five characteristics of a successful action in passing off in *Erven Warnink BV and Another v J Townend & Sons (Hull) Ltd and Another (Advocaat)* (1980):

  (i) A misrepresentation;

  (ii) Made by a trader in the course of trade;

  (iii) To prospective customers of his or to ultimate customers of goods or services supplied by him;

  (iv) Which is calculated to injure the business or goodwill of another trader (in the sense that it is a reasonably foreseeable consequence); and

  (v) This causes actual damage to a business or goodwill of the trader by whom an action is or will be brought.

(b) Lord Oliver reduced the *Advocaat* (1980) test to what is known as the "classic trinity" formulation in *Reckitt & Colman Products Ltd v Borden Inc and Others (Jif Lemon)* (1990):

  (i) The claimant must be able to demonstrate goodwill;

  (ii) There must be a misrepresentation as to the goods or services offered by the defendant; and

  (iii) Actual or likely damage.

Many UK cases follow the *Jif Lemon* (1990) formulation (*e.g. Consorzio del Prosciutto di Parma v Marks & Spencer* (1991) and *BBC v Talksport* (2001)). It also has the advantage of being simpler than the *Advocaat* (1980) test, therefore the *Jif Lemon* (1990) test is the formulation preferred in this work.

ELEMENTS OF PASSING OFF—GOODWILL

Definition of goodwill

Goodwill is a property right (as per Lord Diplock in *Star Industrial v Yap Kwee Kor* (1976)). It is a somewhat amorphous concept, but has been most concisely defined by Lord MacNaughten as "the attractive force that brings in custom" (*The Commissioners of Inland Revenue v Muller & Co* (1901)).

Goodwill is not the same as reputation (this distinction is considered in more detail in the context of territorial considerations, below) and reputation without goodwill is insufficient to support an action for passing off (*Anheuser-Busch v Budejovicky Budvar Narodni Podnik (Budweiser)* (1984) and *Harrods v Harrodian School* (1996)). The distinction between reputation and goodwill was also considered in *BBC v Talksport* (2001). Here, the BBC was the only UK broadcaster entitled to broadcast live Euro 2000 football matches. The BBC objected to Talksport's advertising claim that its Euro 2000 coverage was "live" (Talksport had employed devices such as the addition of pre-recorded sound effects to its broadcasts, giving the false impression that its radio coverage constituted live broadcasts of the matches). The BBC failed in its claim for passing off—while the BBC had a *reputation* as a live broadcaster of sports, a reputation for this activity did not give rise to *protectable goodwill*.

The creation of goodwill

The concept of "trade" is key for establishing goodwill. "Trade" is not, however, restricted to commercial enterprises; non-profitmaking professional bodies have been able to benefit from passing off (*e.g. British Medical Association v Marsh* (1931)), as have charities (*e.g. British Diabetic Association v The Diabetic Society* (1996)).

Although "trade" has been interpreted generously in relation to non-profitmaking bodies, goodwill is seen as a legal property right associated with *business*.

The courts have considered it to be possible to create protectable goodwill within very brief periods of trading. For example, a mere three weeks was sufficient for goodwill to be established in the name MR CHIPPY for a mobile fish and chip van (*Stannard v Reay* (1967)). As to whether goodwill is established, this is decided on a case-by-case basis; there are no set rules. In exceptional circumstances goodwill might be generated by pre-launch activity (*British Broadcasting Corporation v Talbot Motors Co Ltd* (1981)).

The source of the goods or services is vital for establishing goodwill (see the discussion of territorial considerations, below).

It should be noted that goodwill does not necessarily cease when the business ceases trading (*Ad Lib Club v Glanville* (1972)).

Distinctiveness

The claimant must demonstrate the presence of goodwill through signs distinctive of him/her in the public mind. The distinctive element might be a mark, logo, name, an "image" created through advertising, or the get-up of a product. It is important to appreciate that passing off does not *directly* protect names, marks, get-up or other indicia, but the *goodwill* in these.

It is naturally more difficult to build strong goodwill in, for example, a descriptive or generic mark. So, in *McCain International v Country Fair Foods* (1981), the descriptive mark OVEN CHIPS was denied protection as was the descriptive PHONES 4U in *Phones 4u Ltd and another v Phone4u.co.uk Internet Ltd and others* (2005). Yet, establishing goodwill in a descriptive mark is not impossible, in *Antec International v South Western Chicks (Warren) Ltd* (1997), it was established that the words FARM FLUID had come to be associated in the minds of farmers with Antec's product. Provided that those words were capable of being appropriated as a trade term, the claimant had shown that goodwill was established.

Get-up

There are particular difficulties as to the protection of get-up. Only get-up that is distinctive of the claimant as the source of the goods may benefit from the law of passing off. A high threshold has been set by the courts; merely novel or eye-catching packaging is not necessarily distinctive and therefore may not gain protection. Of the cases already considered, *Jif Lemon* (1990) and *McCain International v Country Fair Foods (OVEN CHIPS)* (1981) concern get-up.

Goodwill—territorial and regional considerations

(a) Territorial considerations. It is possible for an overseas trader to have a *reputation* in the UK without actually trading in the UK. The question then arises, has *goodwill* been established in the UK? In *Anheuser-Busch v Budejovicky Budvar Narodni Podnik (Budweiser)* (1984), the answer to this question was no. Here, the US manufacturers of Budweiser failed to demonstrate the necessary goodwill to sustain an action in passing off against a Czech company; American Budweiser was known in the UK, but was only available in US air bases on UK soil.

Only goodwill in the UK is relevant, and this may cause difficulties for the overseas claimant unless the business has managed to establish goodwill in the UK (*Jian Tools v Roderick* (1995)). However, the foreign claimant's customers within the UK must be part of the general public (*Budweiser* (1984)).

(b) Regional considerations. Where a business may enjoy a

local or national goodwill, the geographical area in which this is protected is, theoretically, limited accordingly. In practice, however, the courts have showed some reluctance to award an injunction which is subject to geographical restrictions (*e.g.* as in *Guardian Media Group v Associated Newspapers* (unreported, 2000)).

Shared goodwill

Where parties share goodwill in the same (distinct) product, goodwill attaches to the product and is shared by the manufacturers. Such cases tend to be called "class goodwill cases" and are generally treated as being distinct from "standard" passing off cases. In *Advocaat* (1980), manufacturers of Advocaat (a high quality liqueur made from brandewijn, eggs, yolks and sugar) were held to share goodwill, and, in *Tattinger SA v Allbev Ltd* (1993) producers of champagne (which is precisely defined as sparkling wine produced by the méthode traditionnelle, from grapes produced in the Champagne region of France) were also held to share goodwill. The law in this area has been developed further by the Court of Appeal (*Chocosuisse Union des Fabricants Suisse de Chocolat v Cadbury Ltd* (1999)).

ELEMENTS OF PASSING OFF—MISPREPRESENTATION

The defendant must make a false representation, usually by using the signs that are distinctive of the claimant, which misleads the public. However, the case law demonstrates that misrepresentation can take a variety of forms (*e.g.* the defendant misrepresenting that his goods are those of the claimant; the defendant misrepresenting the claimant's goods as being his own goods; the defendant substituting one product for another in circumstances where the customer is unlikely to notice, and misrepresentation by silence). According to *Spalding v Gamage* (1915), the misrepresentation can be innocent or fraudulent. The misrepresentation must, however, be material (*Miss World v Jame St* (1981)).

The relevance of common field of activity

There is no rule in law stating that the parties must be in a common field of activity for passing off to occur. What is needed, however, is an *association* between the defendant's and claimant's goods. Clearly, although these parties need not share a common field of activity, where this is the case it will be easier for the claimant to demonstrate that there has been a misrepresentation.

For example, in *Stringfellow v McCain* (1984), Peter Stringfellow was unable to prevent STRINGFELLOW from being used in relation to chips. It has been suggested that the diversity between frozen chips and strip clubs was an important factor in this decision.

Class goodwill cases

For class goodwill cases, misrepresentation is not required—there is a line of authority from *Advocaat* (1980) itself to *Choco-suisse* (1999) and *Mars UK Ltd. v Burgess* (2004) to confirm this.

ELEMENTS OF PASSING OFF—DAMAGE

Actual or likely damage must result from the misrepresentation. Possible heads of damage include:

  (i) Direct loss of sales;
 (ii) Dilution;
(iii) Inferiority of the defendant's goods;
 (iv) Injurious association;
  (v) Injury through constant confusion;
 (vi) Loss of licensing opportunity.

DEFENCES AND REMEDIES

Defences

  (i) Failure to establish the elements necessary for a passing off action;
 (ii) Acquiescence or delay;
(iii) Undeserving claimant;
 (iv) Use of own name;
  (v) Honest concurrent user.

Remedies

Remedies are discussed in general in Chapter 2. The following remedies are available for passing off:

(i)   Damages;
(ii) Account of profits;
(iii) Delivery-up or destruction;
(iv) Declaration;
(v)   Injunction.

INTERNET DOMAIN NAMES—PASSING OFF AND TRADE MARKS

Domain names, *e.g. www.soton.ac.uk*, may give rise to both passing off and trade mark issues. Domain names are signs which may be registered as trade marks, providing that they satisfy the usual criteria (see Chapter 5).

The leading case in this area is *British Telecommunications plc v One in a Million Ltd* (1999). Here, One in a Million had registered a number of well-known trade marks with a view to making a profit by selling them on to the relevant brand owners and other third parties. This activity, known as cybersquatting, constituted a false representation to persons who consulted the domain name register that One in a Million was in some way connected or associated with the name registered, and this amounted to passing off. Also, even if TMA 1994, s.10(3) required the use as a trade mark, threats to infringe had been established. Registration of the domain names to exploit the marks' indications of origin, and the threatened disposal of the domain names, was unfair and harmful to the distinctive character and reputation of the trade marks.

The court also introduced the concept of *instrument of fraud*. The defendant's purpose in registering the domain names was to extract money from the owners of the goodwill in those names by the threat, whether express or implied, that the goodwill would be exploited by One in a Million (or by third parties); the domain names were therefore registered as an instruments of fraud.

A more recent decision relating to passing off and domain names is *Phones 4u Ltd and another v Phone4u.co.uk Internet Ltd and others* (2005).

PROBLEMATIC AREAS IN PASSING OFF

Endorsement or sponsorship

Some people may be in a position to exploit their personality or reputation in a particular field by endorsing goods or services. It follows, therefore, that the public may infer from the defendant's representation that the claimant is endorsing the defendant's product or services. It would seem that the claimant's endorsement must be valuable, that the public must infer endorsement from the defendant's representation and that the claimant is "in trade". Following *Stringfellow v McCain* (1984), it seemed that the difficulty in demonstrating that a person is in trade and the requirement of misrepresentation meant that it was difficult to succeed in passing off in cases of endorsement or sponsorship; however, it is possible—as the ruling in *Edmund Irvine v Talksport Ltd* (2002) attests.

Character merchandising

The image of a (usually fictional) character can be very valuable and can be used to sell a range of products and services. In practice, companies rely on a combination of trade marks and contract to protect official character merchandising. With the reform of registered designs, it is now also possible to utilise registered designs in this area (see Chapter 9, below). Historically in the UK, passing off has been unhelpful in character merchandising. The only successful case has been the interim decision in *Mirage Studios v Counter-Feat (Teenage Mutant Ninja Turtles)* (1991).

Deception

Deception is not explicitly required as a necessary characteristic of a passing off action in the *Jif Lemon* (1990) formula. Nevertheless, deception of the public (which, confusingly, is often termed "confusion" in passing off cases) appears to be a key element of the successful passing off action in practice. For example, in *Morning Star v Express Newspaper* (1979) it was said that even "the moron in a hurry" would not be deceived.

7. COPYRIGHT I—SUBSISTENCE OF COPYRIGHT

INTRODUCTION

What is copyright?

Copyright is a property right that subsists in certain works. It is a statutory right giving the copyright owner certain exclusive rights in relation to his/her work, such as the right to make copies of the work, to sell these copies to the public or the right to give a public performance of the work. A range of legislation is pertinent to copyright, with the main UK statute being the Copyright Designs and Patents Act 1988 (hereafter, CDPA 1988).

There are now eight categories of copyright works in the UK:

"Authorial", *"primary"* or *"LDMA"* works (hereafter known as LDMA works):

  (i) Literary works;
 (ii) Dramatic works;
(iii) Musical works; and
 (iv) Artistic works.

"Entrepreneurial", *"secondary"* or *"derivative"* works (hereafter known as secondary works):

   (v) Sound recordings;
  (vi) Films;
 (vii) Broadcasts; and
(viii) The typographical arrangement of published editions (the typography right).

Copyright comes into existence, or subsists, automatically where a *qualifying person* (qualification can also arise from the place of publication) creates a *work* that is *original* (or, for some works, not copied) and *tangible* (or fixed).

QUALIFICATION

Copyright will not subsist in a work unless:

(a) It has been created by a qualifying person (CDPA 1988, s.154).
(b) It was first published in a qualifying country, or transmitted from a qualifying country (CDPA 1988, ss.155 and 156).
(c) In the case of literary, dramatic and musical works, the work must fixed, that is reduced to a material form, in writing or otherwise (CDPA 1988, s.3(2)).

THE EU INFLUENCE ON COPYRIGHT LAW

There is no EU copyright *system* as such, there is merely a series of copyright directives that approximate national law on selected issues within certain areas of copyright law; EU law has, thus, only achieved limited harmonisation of copyright law between member states. Although the EU influence on national law should not be underestimated (indeed, the CDPA 1988 has been variously amended to implement EU directives; the more important EU copyright directives are briefly described in Chapter 1), this chapter, and the subsequent chapter, primarily focuses on the UK statute and UK copyright cases.

COPYRIGHT WORKS

Literary works

CDPA 1988, s.3(1) defines a literary work as being "any work written, spoken or sung, other than a dramatic or musical work". A novel, a poem or instructions on a cereal packet could all equally fall into this category. Additionally, the concept of literary works extends to tables (*e.g.* a bus timetable), compilations (*e.g.* a directory or a CD collation of "The top 20 classical tunes"), and computer programs (see CDPA 1988, s.3(1)(b)) and the preparatory design material for computer programs. Databases (*e.g.* WESTLAW) are regarded as literary works (CDPA 1988, s.3A), but are regarded as being distinct from "compilations" or "tables" (CDPA 1988, s.3(1)(a)).

In essence, any work that can be expressed in print,

irrespective of its quality, will be a literary work (*University of London Press v University Tutorial Press* (1916)).

Dramatic works

CDPA 1988, s.3(1) defines "dramatic work" as including works of dance or mime. In *Norowzian v Arks (No 2)* (1999) it was stated that these terms should be given their natural and ordinary meaning; the implication being that dramatic works are works of *action*. The court also recognised in this case that films may be protected as dramatic works, as dramatic works in themselves and/or as a recording of a dramatic work.

Musical works

A musical work is a work consisting exclusively of musical notes; any words or actions intended to be sung, spoken or performed with the notes are excluded (CDPA 1988, s.3(1)(a)). This means that while the melody of a popular song would constitute a musical work, the lyrics of the song would be a separate copyright work—a literary work.

Artistic works

A wide-ranging definition of "artistic work" is provided by CDPA 1988, s.4. Works of architecture (buildings or models of buildings) are included, but most IP Law courses tend to focus on the remaining types of artistic works. These fall into two categories:

(a) Works protected *irrespective of their artistic merit* (CDPA 1988, s.4(1)(a)). The inevitably difficult questions concerning artistic judgement (*Hi-Tech Autoparts Ltd v Towergate Two Ltd (No 1)* (2002)) can therefore be ignored for the following artistic works:
    (i) Graphic works, *i.e.* paintings, drawings, diagrams, maps, charts, plans, engravings, etchings, lithographs, woodcuts or similar works.
    It should be noted that as there is no requirement of artistic merit; functional items may be graphic works. Further, items used in the production of such works may themselves be protected, for example many graphic works are produced from engravings

which may themselves be copyright works. This is an area where design law and copyright overlap, see Chapter 9 for further information.

(ii) Photographs.

(iii) Sculptures. The protection of functional objects, such as a cast, is, again, problematic here. Famously in a New Zealand case, *Wham-O Manufacturing Co v Lincoln Industries Ltd* (1985) a wooden model of a Frisbee used in manufacturing was held to be a sculpture. The modern UK position is almost certainly more restrictive, as objects will not now be protected as sculptures where they are not made for the purposes of sculpture (*J&S Davis (Holdings) Ltd v Wright Health Group* (1988)).

(iv) Collages. Collages are artistic or functional visual arrangements produced by affixing two or more items together. Intrinsically ephemeral arrangements (for example, the composition of a photograph as in *Creation Records Ltd v News Group Newspapers Ltd* (1997)) are deemed not to be collages.

(b) Artistic works *required to be of a certain quality* (CDPA 1988, s.4(1)(c)), *i.e.* works of artistic craftsmanship. Few works can meet the standards of artistic craftsmanship, as they must be *both* of artistic quality *and* the result of craftsmanship (*George Hensher Ltd v Restawhile* (1976)). These principles were further developed into a two-part test for artistic craftsmanship in *Merlet v Mothercare plc* (1986), first, did the creation of the work involve craftsmanship in the sense that skill and pride was invested in its manufacture? Second, does the work have aesthetic appeal, and did an artist create it? In the view of this author, this is still the current test for CDPA 1988, s.4(1)(c), but students should be aware that subsequent cases (*e.g. Guild v Eskandar* (2001)) have created some confusion as to whether the *Merlet* test has been modified or replaced.

Sound recordings

A sound recording is a reproducible recording of either:

(i) Sounds where there is no underlying copyright work (*e.g.* birdsong, the sound of waves) (CDPA 1988, s.5A(1)(a)); or

(ii) A recording of the whole or any part of a literary, dramatic or musical work (CDPA 1988, s.5A(1)(b)).

The format of the recording (vinyl record, audio or videotape, DVD, etc.) is irrelevant.

Film

CDPA 1988, s.5B(1) provides that a film is a reproducible recording of a moving image on any medium (*e.g.* celluloid or digital recordings). It is the recording itself that is protected, rather than the subject matter that has been recorded, but it should be borne in mind that a film may also be protected as a dramatic work. Film soundtracks are taken to be part of the film itself (CDPA 1988, s.5B(2)).

Broadcasts

While the initial definition of "broadcast" is a broad one, there are some restrictions as to the extent to which broadcasts via the Internet (commonly known as a "webcasts") are protected as copyright works. According to CDPA 1988, s.6(1), copyright subsists in:

(a) The electronic transmission of sounds, visual images and other information that are transmitted for simultaneous lawful reception by the public. This includes transmissions on terrestrial, cable or satellite television and transmissions on radio stations, where these are lawfully received. Excluded from this definition are (i) "on demand" broadcasts, (ii) illegally received broadcasts, such as "pirate" decoding of encrypted subscription satellite televisions services by non-subscribers and (iii) private transmissions, *e.g.* telephone calls, emails or intranet transmissions; or
(b) The electronic transmission of sounds, visual images and other information that are transmitted at a time determined by the transmitter, for presentation to the public.

CDPA 1988, s.6(1A) excludes Internet transmissions from the definition of "broadcast" subject to three exceptions (which can be seen as being intended to ensure that where what might be termed "conventional" broadcasting activity occurs, that it is protected):

(i) CDPA 1988, s.6(1A)(a) provides that where there is a webcast that is simultaneous with another broadcast (*e.g.* where there is *simultaneous webcast and broadcast* by digital radio stations), the former is also protected as a broadcast;

(ii) CDPA 1988, s.6(1A)(b) provides that where there is a webcast concurrent with a live event (*e.g.* where there is a *live webcast* of a concert), the webcast will be protected as a broadcast; and

(iii) CDPA 1988, s.6(1A)(c) provides that where the webcast comprises the transmission of moving images or sounds forming part of a programme service offered by the transmitter and transmitted at a time scheduled by the transmitter (*e.g.* a *scheduled transmission* of an Internet soap opera that is *not transmitted on any other media*), here the webcast will be protected as a broadcast.

It should be noted that <u>before October 31, 2003</u> the concept of "broadcast" was defined more narrowly under the CDPA 1988; indeed, before that date distinction was drawn between wireless transmissions (broadcasts) and cable programmes (which comprised a separate category of copyright work). This fact is drawn to the attention of the student simply because copyright cases, articles and texts relating to the law before the implementation of the Information Society directive in 2003 will be out of date on this issue.

The typography right

CDPA 1988, s.8 affords protection to the typography, that is the layout, of published editions of literary, dramatic and musical works (although these underlying works need not themselves be the subject of copyright protection). The leading authority on typographical arrangement copyright is *Newspaper Licensing Agency Ltd v Marks & Spencer plc* (2001).

COPYRIGHT WORKS: THE IDEA/EXPRESSION DICHOTOMY

There is no copyright in ideas; copyright subsists in the *tangible expression* of ideas, <u>not</u> in the ideas themselves. In America this is referred to as the idea/expression dichotomy. This principle can be helpful in understanding UK copyright law, but should not be taken too literally, as while it is clear that mere ideas cannot be protected by copyright (*e.g.* catchphrases and other features of a game show in *Green v New Zealand Broadcasting Corp* (1989) or editing techniques and styles in *Norowzian v Arks (No 2)* (1999)), the following points should be noted:

(i) What might be termed "highly developed ideas", *e.g.* an early draft of a textbook, would be protected by copyright, as are preparatory design materials for computer programs (CDPA 1988, s.3(1)(c)); and

(ii) Copyright cannot be circumvented by selectively altering the expression of a copyright work in the process of reproducing it (*i.e.* infringement is not limited to an exact reproduction of how the work was expressed. As noted in Chapter 8, infringement will be found were there is a *substantial taking* of a copyright work)

ORIGINALITY

CDPA 1988, s.1 requires that literary, dramatic, musical and artistic works be "original". The originality requirement <u>only applies to LDMA works</u>, there is no such requirement for the secondary copyright works, although it is clear that no copyright will subsist in secondary copyright works that merely reproduce existing secondary works (*e.g.* see CDPA 1988, s.5A(2)).

LDMA works must be original in the sense that they originate with the author (*University of London Press v University Tutorial Press* (1916)). This is a minimal qualitative requirement: original works need not be inventive or original and a wide range of material has been held to be original, from coupons for football pools (*Ladbrokes v William Hill* (1964)) to a compilation of broadcasting programmes (*Independent Television Publications Ltd and the BBC v Time Out Ltd* (1984)).

Expending skill and judgement in creating an LDMA work usually suffices to deem the work original. Mere copying cannot confer originality (*Interlego AG v Tyco* (1989)), the pre-existing work must be developed or embellished in some way for copyright to subsist in the new work (although such activity may still constitute copyright infringement).

Alternatively, the mere expenditure of effort or labour (the so-called "sweat of the brow" test for originality) has sometimes been said to be sufficient to confer originality, but in practice some minimum element of skill or judgement is also usually required. Certainly in the past, "sweat of the brow" has been deemed insufficient, for example in *Cramp v Smythson* (1944) it was held that the generic nature of commonplace diary material left no room for judgement in selection and arrangement, therefore the resultant works were not original. Originality has also been held to require more than "competent draftsmanship" (*Interlego v Tyco* (1988)). Commonly, databases and computer programs were the subject matter of "sweat of the brow" concerns. The standard test for originality would seem less relevant to databases and computer programs now, given that both are now subject to a higher statutory standard of originality (see below). It should be noted that databases may, in addition or instead of copyright protection, be protected by the *sui generis* database right (see Chapter 8) and that computer programs may, in addition to or instead of copyright protection, benefit from protection under patent law as part of a computer-implemented invention (see Chapter 3).

Higher standards of originality: computer programs and databases

As a result of two European Directives, namely the Directive on the legal protection of databases (Directive 96/9/EC) and the Computer Directive (Directive 91/250/EEC), both computer programs and databases must be original in the sense that they are the author's own intellectual creation. This is a higher standard of originality than that of "skill, labour and judgement". The higher standard of originality is made explicit in the CDPA 1988 for databases (CDPA 1988, s.3A(2)) but, interestingly, no equivalent provision was introduced for computer programs.

Originality and the *de minimis* principle

Does copyright subsist in very short works? *Exxon Corporation v Exxon Ind* (1982), where the invented word "Exxon" was denied copyright protection, is often cited to support the proposition that a *de minimis* principle applies in copyright law, *i.e.* that some things are too small to be deemed copyright works. However, the authority for this is not entirely clear; decisions in this area often seem motivated by policy considerations rather than the brevity of the alleged copyright work. For example, the fact that "Exxon" would be more appropriately protected by other intellectual property rights, such as trade mark law or passing off may have been an underlying consideration in the decision in *Exxon Corporation v Exxon Ind* (1982). In reality, the concept of originality (as well as other established copyright notions such as the idea/expression dichotomy) is more than equal to the task of objecting to truly trivial works—a separate *de minimis* principle may not be necessary and may be actively confusing.

FIXATION AND TANGIBILITY

Copyright does not subsist in literary, dramatic or musical works until they are recorded in writing or otherwise (CDPA 1988, s.3(2)). This pragmatic requirement is known as "fixation". Usually such works will be fixed by the author, but fixation by a third party (with or without the author's permission) is also possible (CDPA 1988, s.3(3)).

Other copyright works are not subject to the fixation requirement. This is usually unproblematic as films, sound recordings, broadcasts, cable programs and typography are inherently tangible works. Problems may arise with artistic works where their form is transitory or otherwise lack permanence. While there is no statutory requirement of fixation for artistic works, the courts do in fact appear to require that artistic works are tangible and permanent (see *Merchandising Corp of America v Harpbond* (1983) and *Komesaroff v Mickle* (1988)).

OWNERSHIP OF COPYRIGHT AND THE EMPLOYEE AUTHOR

The basic rule is that the first owner of copyright in a work is the person who created the work, the author, (CDPA 1988, s.11(1)). A major exception to this rule is CDPA 1988, s.11(2), which provides that where a person creates an LDMA work in the course of employment, the employer is the first owner of any copyright in the work, subject to an agreement to the contrary (such an agreement could be written, oral or implied from conduct). There are also special provisions for Crown use, Parliamentary copyright and copyright for certain international organisations (CDPA 1988, s.11(3)).

Who is the author?

Not only is correct identification of the author important for determining who is the first owner of a copyright work, it is important in respect of infringement, moral rights, and determining the duration of the copyright term. The author is the person who creates the work (CDPA 1988, s.9(1)), the person whose skill, labour and effort brings the work into existence. It therefore follows, for example, that the person who writes a literary work is usually the author of that work. However, if he/she were taking dictation, the speaker would be the author, not the writer, as the writer in dictation is merely acting as an amanuensis (*Donoghue v Allied Newspapers* (1938), but *cf. Walter v Lane* (1900)). Identifying the author is usually a straightforward task and the table below summarises the standard authorship position:

COPYRIGHT WORK	PERSON(S) USUALLY TAKEN TO BE THE AUTHOR(S)
Literary work	The writer (CDPA 1988, s.9(1))
Dramatic work	The writer (CDPA 1988, s.9(1))
Musical work	The composer (CDPA 1988, s.9(1))
Artistic work	The artist (CDPA 1988, s.9(1))
Computer generated LDMA works	The person operating the computer (CDPA 1988, s.9(3))
Sound recordings	The producer (CDPA 1988, s.9(2)(aa))
Films	The producer and principal director (CDPA 1988, s.9(2)(ab))
Broadcasts	The broadcaster (CDPA 1988, s.9(2)(b))
Typography right	The publisher (CDPA 1988, s.9(2)(d)).
Any work where the identity of the author is unknown	A work of unknown authorship (CDPA 1988, ss.9(4) and (5))

Joint authorship

Complications arise where more than one person is involved in the creation of a work. Determining whether a person's contribution is sufficient for them to be deemed an author and whether joint authorship or co-authorship is present demands careful consideration of the facts. A person who suggests a subject to a poet is not the author of the resultant poem (*e.g.* see *Tate v Thomas* (1921)). Merely supplying ideas is insufficient for joint authorship (*Wiseman v George Weidenfeld and Nicholson Ltd and Donaldson* (1985)); an integral role in the expression of those ideas is required, as in *Cala Homes v Alfred McAlpine Homes* (1995).

Joint authorship (CDPA 1988, s.10(1)) arises when the efforts of two or more authors are indistinguishable (*e.g. Cala Homes v Alfred McAlpine Homes* (1995)).

Ownership and employees

Where LDMA works or films are created by employees, the first owner of copyright in these works will vest in the employer when (CDPA 1988, s.11(2)):

(a) The work was created by an employee (see *Stephenson Jordan & Harrison v MacDonald* (1952));
(b) It was created during the course of employment (see *Noah v Shuba* (1991)); and
(c) There is no agreement to the contrary.

The distinction between a contract of service and a contract for services is important for identifying who is an employee. Persons employed as consultants or persons commissioned to produce copyright works are not employees and therefore not subject to CDPA 1988, s.11(2), so the position as to ownership of copyright must thus be made clear via contract. Any transfer of copyright must be in signed writing (CDPA 1988, s.90(3)). It is possible to deal in future copyrights (CDPA 1988, s.91), but again, assignment must be in signed writing (CDPA 1988, s.91(1)).

---

8. COPYRIGHT II—INFRINGEMENT, REMEDIES AND NEIGHBOURING RIGHTS

INTRODUCTION TO INFRINGEMENT

Infringement may take two forms, *primary* infringement and *secondary* infringement. Primary infringement occurs where restricted acts are carried out without the permission of the copyright owner. Secondary infringement is concerned with large-scale infringements taking place with actual or constructive knowledge, *i.e.* forms of piracy. Nevertheless, most secondary infringements will be based on an earlier primary infringement; for example, dealing in infringing copies will usually be based on an earlier infringement of the primary reproduction rights.

The restricted acts

The copyright owner has the exclusive right to do certain restricted acts in relation to his/her copyright work. *Primary infringement* (CDPA 1988, ss.17–21) occurs where any person (directly or indirectly) carries out, or purports to authorise another to carry out, any of these restricted acts, without the permission of the copyright owner, in relation to the whole or a substantial part of the copyright work (CDPA 1988, s.16(2)). The restricted acts are (CDPA 1988, s.16(1)):

(a) To copy the work (known as the reproduction right);
(b) To issue copies of the work to the public (known as the distribution right);
(c) To rent or lend the work to the public (known as the rental and lending rights);
(d) To perform, show or play the work in public (known as the public performance right);
(e) To communicate the work to the public (known as the communication right); and
(f) To make an adaptation of the work, or to do any of the above acts in relation to an adaptation of the work (known as the adaptation right).

Secondary infringement (CDPA 1988, ss.22–26) usually occurs where there is commercial use of a copyright work; it concerns the commission of certain acts, without the permission of the copyright owner, with respect to infringing copies (CDPA 1988, s.27) or the means of producing infringing copies. Unlike primary infringement, secondary infringement requires that the infringer knows or has reason to believe that he/she is dealing with infringing copies of a work. Secondary infringement concerns:

(a) Importing an infringing copy;
(b) Possessing an infringing copy;
(c) Selling, exhibiting or distributing an infringing copy;

(d) Dealing with items that are used for the making of infringing copies of specific works; and

(e) Permitting premises to be used for an infringing performance or providing apparatus for such performances.

PRIMARY INFRINGEMENT

Taking the whole or a substantial part of a copyright work

This is a key element of primary infringement. First, the claimant's copyright work must be the *source* of the allegedly infringing work (*Francis Day & Hunter v Bron* (1963)). This causal connection may be indirect (*Plix Products v Winstone* (1986)) or even subconscious, but if the allegedly infringing work was created independently it will not infringe (*Francis Day & Hunter v Bron* (1963)).

Secondly, the *extent* of the taking is important. When the whole of a work has been taken for the purposes of carrying out a restricted act (*e.g.* for copying), infringement is straightforward. More difficult is where part of the claimant's copyright work is taken for these purposes, as it then must be decided whether the taking is substantial.

The CDPA 1988 provides no definition of "substantial", but some guidance can be found in the case law. It is clear that one assesses *both* the *quality* and the *quantity* of the taking from the claimant's work in deciding whether there has been a substantial taking (*Ladbroke Football Ltd v William Hill (Football) Ltd* (1964)). Some attempts have been made to suggest a percentage test (*i.e.* "where x per cent of the claimant's work is taken by the defendant, then that is a substantial taking"), but this is unhelpful and ignores the qualitative aspect of the approach to this issue. Factors that do seem to influence the decisions on this issue include:

(i) The distinctiveness of the portion taken. For example, in *Hawkes v Paramount Films* (1934), 28 bars of a song amounted to a substantial taking of the underlying musical work, but these bars amounted to a highly recognisable portion of that song;

(ii) The nature of the copyright work appears to have some relevance, as the dividing line between idea and expression appears to be intrinsically clearer in some copyright works than for others. For example, when a melody brings to mind that of an earlier song, this is often because it is substantially the same as that of the earlier song. As taking relatively small portions of musical works can infringe (*e.g. Hawkes v Paramount Films* (1934)), this may well constitute infringement. In contrast, establishing infringement may be more problematic in relation to artistic works. Two artistic works may share recognisable *concepts*, but as there is much scope to express them in a different way this may not be enough to constitute infringement (see *e.g. Bauman v Fussell* (1953)); and

(iii) The timing of the taking. In most cases, a substantial portion of a copyright work will be taken at a particular point of time, and taking will be a single event. It is more difficult to establish that a number of small takings (individually insubstantial, but significant when added up) over a period of time constitutes copyright infringement (*Electronic Techniques v Critchley* (1997)).

Interesting issues may be found in relation to the following activities:

(i) Sampling. In the music industry, the process of taking a small but recognisable part of a recording and repeating it, together with other material, to form a new recording may result in a new copyright work. However, where substantial portions of other copyright works have been taken, this will still constitute infringement.

(ii) Computer programs. A computer program might be protected by patent law (see Chapter 3) and/or by copyright as an original literary work. Where the whole or a substantial part of an original program's code is copied, a finding of infringement is usually straightforward (*e.g. Ibcos v Barclay* (1994)). More problematic is where the structure, function or appearance of a program is taken; such issues are considered in *Ibcos v Barclay* (1994) and *Cantor Fitzgerald v Tradition* (2000).

Authorising infringement

Purporting to authorise any of the restricted acts also constitutes primary infringement (CDPA 1988, s.16(2)), *e.g. MCA Records v Charly* (2002). The main principles of authorising infringement are set out in *CBS v Amstrad* (1988).

Infringement of the reproduction right

Reproducing (copying) the whole or a substantial part of an LDMA work in any material form without the permission of the copyright owner constitutes infringement. Reproduction here includes electronic storage (CDPA 1988, s.17(2)) and, for example, taking a photograph of a painting or making a drawing of a sculpture (CDPA 1988, s.17(3)). What is not included is use of design documents or models recording a copyright work (other than an artistic work) to produce an article (CDPA 1988, s.51(1)). It is also not an infringement to make a three-dimensional work from written instructions (*e.g. Foley v Elliot* (1982)). There are also specific provisions relating to secondary works (CDPA 1988, ss.179(4) and (5)).

Infringement of the distribution right

The copyright owner has the exclusive right of first distribution, within the EEA, of copies of the work, subject to the doctrine of exhaustion (CDPA 1988, s.18). See *Infabrics v Jaytex* (1982).

Infringement of the rental and lending rights

This applies to LDMA works (other than works of architecture or applied art), films and sound recordings (CDPA 1988, s.18A). It is an infringement to rent or lend copies of such works without the permission of the copyright owner.

Infringement of the public performance right

CDPA 1988, s.19 provides that any work, other than an artistic work, is infringed by its performance in public, where the copyright owner has not given permission. A performance could be visual and/or acoustic and be "live" and/or recorded (*e.g.* playing a recorded song). The courts are clear that performances in non-domestic contexts constitute performances in public, *e.g.* performances in a factory constituted a public performance in *Ernest Turner v PRS* (1943). However, performances to sizeable or paying audiences in a semi-domestic scenario are more problematic. See *Jennings v Stephens* (1936) and *PRS v Harlequin* (1979).

Infringement of the communication right

Literary, dramatic, musical and artistic works, sound recordings, films and broadcasts will be infringed where the work is broadcast or electronically transmitted to members of the public without the permission of the copyright owner (CDPA 1988, s.20). This would include making a song available for unauthorised download on a website.

Infringement of the adaptation right

Literary, dramatic and musical works are infringed where they are adapted without the permission of the copyright owner (CDPA 1988, 21(3)). This includes translation and transcribing, such as a novel being turned into a play, in certain circumstances (CDPA 1988, s.21). It is clear that this extends to adaptation of computer programs (CDPA 1988, s.21(3)(ab)) and many adaptations may also involve copying.

SECONDARY INFRINGEMENT

Where making an article involved copyright infringement, that article will be an "infringing copy"—commercial dealings in such copies often also constitute secondary infringement. Secondary infringement occurs where a person, without the licence of the owner and with actual or constructive knowledge (this is assessed objectively), does any of the following:

(i) Imports an infringing copy (CDPA 1988, s.22);

(ii) Possesses an infringing copy (CDPA 1988, s.23);

(iii) Sells, exhibits or distributes an infringing copy (CDPA 1988, s.23);

(iv) Deals with items that are used for the making of infringing copies of specific works (CDPA 1988, s.24); and

(v) Permits premises to be used for an infringing performance (CDPA 1988, s.25) or provides apparatus for such performances (CDPA 1988, s.26).

TECHNOLOGICAL PROTECTION MEASURES AND ELECTRONIC RIGHTS MANAGEMENT INFORMATION

A relatively new feature of the CDPA 1988 is the protection that it affords to so-called technological protection measures (TPMs) and electronic rights management. Although it is difficult to categorise this area of copyright law (is it a form of secondary infringement or is it a type of neighbouring right?), it is convenient, as the permitted acts have particular import for the TPM provisions, for this area of copyright law to be discussed here.

The circumvention of technological protection measures (TPMs)

Where TPMs are applied to copyright works (and sometimes where applied to the *generis* database right and to rights in performance) and a TPM is circumvented, this can give rise to civil liability and/or criminal prosecution. What is protected here is copy-protection techniques that are designed to prevent or restrict unauthorised acts in relation to copyright works such as encryption, digital watermarking, digital fingerprinting. Such copy-protection techniques are valuable to copyright proprietors as they can offer practical ways to dissuade unauthorised copying, as TPMs place technological barriers to, for example, the unauthorised use of copyright works via peer-to-peer file sharing.

The rationale for protecting TPMs is that copy-protection mechanisms can be circumvented, and therefore copyright law needs to protect them. This has been achieved by the introduction of civil remedies against the act of circumvention as well as the making and dealing in circumvention devices and the provision of circumvention services (CDPA 1988, ss.296(2), 296ZA(3) and 296ZD). Criminal sanctions (CDPA 1988, s.296ZB) are only available against the making and dealing in circumvention devices and the provision of circumvention services.

It should be noted that the CDPA 1988 deals with circumventions of technical devices relating to computer programs (CDPA 1988, s.296; *Sony Computer Entertainment Inc v Edmunds* (2002), which was decided under a similar previous provision, probably still applies here) separately from the circumvention of TPMs applied to all other copyright works (CDPA 1988, ss.296ZA–296ZF).

This is a very complex area of copyright law and is likely to prove to be difficult to apply in practice. It is also a highly controversial area, both in law (because CDPA 1988, ss.296 and 296ZA have had the effect of directly protecting TPMs when applied to copyright works) and in practice (because copy-protected material has often reduced functionality, *e.g.* some forms of copy-protection prevent CDs from being played on a computer. While CDPA 1988, s.296ZE is meant to provide some assistance here, the mechanism provided for the intervention by the Secretary of State where permitted acts appear to have been prejudiced is unlikely to be effective).

Electronic rights management information

Electronic rights management (ERM) (also known as electronic copyright management (ECM) or digital rights management (DRM)) is, in practice, difficult to define. It can concern systems for encrypting or otherwise securing electronic material (so it may have TPM elements), or it may relate to the identification, tracking and monitoring of the use of electronic material content. In all cases, ERM can be used to manage the distribution and exploitation of material, including that of copyright works. ERM can also be used to aid the maintenance of the confidential status of material.

In essence, CDPA 1988, s.296ZG provides that a person engaging in the unauthorised removal or alteration of rights management information associated with a copyright work (or public performances or the *sui generis* database right) that induces, enables, conceals or facilitates copyright infringement (where there is constructive knowledge) will be liable.

DEFENCES

CDPA 1988, s.16(4) provides that the restricted acts are themselves subject to certain defences, termed "permitted acts" (CDPA 1988, ss.28–76) and the copyright licensing provisions (CDPA 1988, s.116 onwards). Discussion of the latter is beyond the scope of this work. Activities falling within the permitted acts will not infringe copyright. There are a large number of permitted acts and a simplified presentation of the main permitted acts is given in the following table:

PERMITTED ACT	OUTLINE OF SCOPE OF PERMITTED ACT
Fair dealing for the purposes of **research** (CDPA 1988, s.29(1)) **and private study** (CDPA 1988, s.29(1C))	Fair dealing for research for *non-commercial* (see *Sillitoe v McGraw-Hill* (1983)) purposes applies to LDMA works and to the typography right. Fair dealing for private study applies to LDMA works and the typography right, but copying by a person other than the researcher or student him/herself is normally outside this permitted act (see CDPA 1988, s.29(3)).
Fair dealing for the purposes of **criticism or review** (CDPA 1988, s.30(1))	Applies to all copyright works that have been made available to the public and to the performance of such works, but a sufficient acknowledgement of the title and author of the copyright work is required. See *Pro Sieben v Carlton* (1999). See also *IPC Media Limited v News Group Newspapers Limited* (2005).
Fair dealing for the purposes **of reporting current events** (CDPA 1988, s.30(2))	Applies to all copyright works except photographs. The use must relate to a current event, even where older materials are used. Acknowledgement is required unless it is a sound recording, film, broadcast or cable programme. See *BBC v BSB* (1992) and *Newspaper Licensing Agency Ltd v Marks & Spencer plc* (2001). See also *IPC Media Limited v News Group Newspapers Limited* (2005).
Incidental inclusion (CDPA 1988, s.31)	Incidental inclusion of copyright material in an artistic work, sound recording, film, broadcast or cable programme will not infringe copyright. The deliberate inclusion of such copyright material does not preclude benefit from this defence (see *Football Association Premier League Ltd v Panini UK* (2004)), but *per* CDPA 1988, s.31(3), where musical works are deliberately included, this will constitute infringement.
The **visual impairment** permitted acts (CDPA 1988, ss.31A–31F and s.74)	Single copies for personal use (CDPA 1988, s.31A) or multiple copies (CDPA 1988, s.31B) of LDMA works (and the typography right) may be made in order to make such a work accessible to the visually impaired, subject to certain conditions. CDPA 1988, s.74 allows for the copying or modification of broadcasts for individuals with impaired hearing, other physical handicaps and mental handicaps.

The **educational exceptions** (CDPA 1988, ss.32–36A)	Various narrow exceptions for educational institutions.
The **library and archive exemptions** (CDPA 1988, s.37–44A)	Various narrow exceptions for libraries and archives.
Making **back up copies** of computer programs (CDPA 1988, s.50A)	This will not infringe when carried out by a lawful user for a permitted purpose.
Decompilation of a computer program for the purposes of achieving interoperability (CDPA 1988, s.50B)	This will not infringe where the decompilation is for the purposes of achieving interoperability.
The **spoken word exception** (CDPA 1988, s.58)	Where the speaker withholds permission, use of records of spoken words for certain purposes is permitted where certain requirements are satisfied.
Recording transmissions for **time shifting** (CDPA 1988, s.70)	Recording a broadcast or cable programme, *e.g.* on a video or a cassette tape, is permitted for private and domestic use where it is for the purposes of time shifting.
The **public interest defence** (CDPA 1988, s.171(3))	Applies to all copyright works. The courts may refuse to enforce copyright, either entirely or in part, where there is a public interest in publication (even where the information is confidential—see *Lion Labs v Evans* (1985)) or any other rule of law is relevant, *e.g.* non-derogation from grant in *British Leyland v Armstrong* (1986). On the so-called public interest defence, in addition to the *Lion Labs* decision there are two contradictory Court of Appeal judgements—*Hyde Park v Yelland* (2000) and *Paddy Ashdown MP v Telegraph Group Ltd* (2001). See also "Copyright—the impact of the Human Rights Act 1998", below.

REMEDIES AND SANCTIONS

Remedies are discussed in general in Chapter 2. The following remedies are available for copyright infringement:

(i) Damages (CDPA 1988, s.96), but innocent infringement does not give rise to a right to damages (CDPA 1988, s.97). However, additional damages (CDPA 1988, s.97(2)(a)) may be available. These are calculated having regard to all the circumstances, including the flagrancy of the breach and any benefit accruing to the defendant from the infringement;

(ii) Injunctions (CDPA 1988, s.96) and orders for discovery against ISPs (CDPA 1988, s.97A);

(iii) Account of profits (CDPA 1988, s.96);

(iv) Seizure of infringing copies (CDPA 1988, s.100);

(v) Delivery up of infringing copies and articles specifically designed or adapted for the making copies (CDPA 1988, s.99); and

(vi) Criminal sanctions (CDPA 1988, ss.107–108).

Moral rights (discussed below) are protected as a breach of statutory duty (CDPA 1988, s.103(1)). Damages are available and injunctions may be obtained, but, as per CDPA 1988, s.103(2), injunctions may be unavailable in relation to the integrity right where the defendant has made a disclaimer disassociating the author from the treatment of the work at issue.

COPYRIGHT—THE IMPACT OF THE HUMAN RIGHTS ACT 1988

An individual's right to privacy and the right to freedom of expression (these are considered in Chapter 4, above) may be relevant to the enforcement of copyright. For example, they may be relevant to the public interest defence or relate to issues of fair dealing. *Hyde Park v Yelland* (2000) and *Paddy Ashdown MP v Telegraph Group Ltd* (2001) are among the cases that should be considered here.

MORAL RIGHTS

These are personal rights (CDPA 1988, s.94) conferred upon the author of primary copyright works and the directors of films and are quite separate from the economic interests in the work. There are four moral rights—the right of paternity, the right to integrity, the right to object to false attribution and the right to privacy in photographs and films. These are very specific rights and all may be waived by the author (CDPA 1988, s.87).

Paternity

Authors of LDMA works and directors of films have the right to be identified as such, in certain situations (CDPA 1988, s.77). In order to benefit, the author/director must assert his/her right (CDPA 1988, ss.77(1) and 78) and there are a variety of exceptions (CDPA 1988, s.79).

Integrity

CDPA 1988, ss.80–83 concern the right of authors of LDMA works and directors of films to object to the derogatory treatment of their work: that is, that the work has been added to, altered or deleted (CDPA 1988, s.80(2)) in such a way to amount to a distortion, mutilation or otherwise prejudicial treatment. CDPA 1988, s.81 sets out the exceptions to infringement. Cases such as *Tidy v Trustees of the Natural History Museum* (1996) illustrate that it can be difficult to succeed with a claim of breach of the integrity right.

False attribution

Any person has the right for LDMA works and films not to be incorrectly attributed to him/her (CDPA 1988, ss.84–86). The attribution may be express, but it can also be implied. See, for example, *Clark v Associated Newspapers* (1998).

Privacy in photos and films

The commissioner of photographs or a film has certain rights of privacy in relation to these where they are commissioned for private purposes (CDPA 1988, s.85). *E.g. Mail Newspapers v Express Newspapers* (1987).

THE DURATION OF COPYRIGHT AND NEIGHBOURING RIGHTS

The rules governing duration of copyright are complicated by a number of factors, principally that duration differs according to the category of copyright and the fact that the duration for many such works were changed by the Term Directive (Directive 93/98/EEC). The implementation of the Directive meant that the term of many existing copyright works were extended and some works in which copyright had previously lapsed were revived. The following table is a simplified guide to the main rules on copyright duration and also the duration of the neighbouring rights (the latter are introduced below):

RIGHT	DURATION
Copyright in **LDMA works** (CDPA 1988, s.12(2))	70 years from the end of the calendar year in which the author dies (life plus 70 years).

Copyright in **works of joint authorship** (CDPA 1988, s.12(8))	70 years after the death of the last surviving author.
Copyright in **LDMA works of unknown authorship** (CDPA 1988, ss.12(3)–(5))	70 years from the date it was made, or, if during that period the work was made available to the public, 70 years from when it was made so available. If the author's name is discovered before this 70-year period expires and the author is still alive, then the term is extended to the normal copyright period of life plus 70 years.
Copyright in **computer generated LDMA works** (CDPA 1988, s.12(7))	50 years from the end of the year in which the work was made.
Copyright in **films** (CDPA 1988, s.13B)	70 years from the end of the calendar year in which the last of the following persons dies: <ul><li>the principal director of the film</li><li>the author of the film screenplay</li><li>the dialogue author, or</li><li>the film music composer.</li></ul> If the identity of these persons is unknown, then protection is for 70 years from the year in which the film was made, but where the film is made available to the public within this period, it becomes 70 years from the end of the year in which the film was made available to the public.
Copyright in **sound recordings** (CDPA 1988, s.13A)	50 years from the making of the sound recording, or, if released during that period, 50 years from its release.
Copyright in **broadcasts** and **cable programs** (CDPA 1988, s.14)	50 years from the making of the broadcast or from when the programme was first included in a cable program.
Copyright in the **typographical arrangement of published editions** (CDPA 1988, s.15)	25 years from the year of first publication.
Crown Copyright (CDPA 1988, s.163(3)) in LDMA works	125 years from the year in which it was made or 50 years from the date it was commercially published, whichever is the lower.
Parliamentary Copyright (CDPA 1988, s.165(3))	50 years from the year in which the work was made.
Moral rights (CDPA 1988, s.86)	The integrity and paternity rights last for as long as copyright. The right to object to false attribution endures for the author's lifetime plus 20 years.
Performers rights (CDPA 1988, s.191(2))	50 years from the performance or the release of the recording of the performance.

Sui generis database right (Database Regulations 1997, s.30).	15 years from the making of the database.
Public lending right	This lasts as long as the underlying copyright.

NEIGHBOURING RIGHTS

This is a general term taken to refer to rights outside copyright law, but related to it, including performers' rights, the *sui generis* database right and the public lending right. Each is very briefly described below.

Performers' rights

There are a number of rights intended to protect the performers of dramatic works, musical works, some literary works and "variety acts" (CDPA 1988, s.180(2)):

  (i) The right to authorise the recording of a live performance made for various commercial purposes (CDPA 1988, s.182).
 (ii) Performers are given certain property rights in their performances (CDPA 1988, ss.182A–C).
(iii) Performers have certain right to remuneration (CDPA 1988, ss.182D and 191G).

The *sui generis* database right

An original database may be protected as a literary work (see Chapter 7) and/or via a *sui generis* database right (the Copyright and Rights in Database Regulations 1997, hereafter the Database Regulations). Databases, therefore, have a two-level system of protection, the main features of which are compared in the following table:

Copyright protection of databases	Protection via the *sui generis* database right
Subsists in databases that are original (*i.e.* the intellectual creation of the author).	Subsists in databases whose compilation involved a substantial monetary, technical or manpower investment in obtaining, verifying or presenting the database's contents.

Protects the arrangement of the data.	Protects the data (contents) as infringement occurs with non-consensual extraction or re-utilization of the whole or a substantial part of the database.
The usual copyright defences apply (see "Permitted Acts", above).	Lawful users of publicly available databases (*e.g.* subscribers) may extract and re-utilize insubstantial parts of the database for any purpose. Exceptions are also made for fair dealing, public lending and there are other defences that echo those provided for copyright in CDPA 1988, 45–50.
Full literary copyright term of protection—life of the author plus 70 years.	15 years term of protection, but further 15 year terms will be afforded where there has been a substantial change to the content of a database.

Guidance to the scope of protection afforded by the *sui generis* database right can be found in a number of national court referrals to the ECJ, chief among them *British Horseracing Board v William Hill Organisation* (2004). The impact of these rulings is, at present, uncertain but on the issue of infringement:

(i) Although the ECJ indicated that the concept of "extraction" should be given a broad meaning, catching all acts of appropriation of database content and both direct and indirect appropriation (further, the intent of the appropriator(s) is irrelevant and non-commercial use of appropriated material will still infringe);

(ii) Mere consultation of a protected database does not constitute infringement; and

(iii) On the requirement that the extraction or re-utilisation is required to occur in relation to the whole or a substantial part of the protected database; the concept of "substantial" has been interpreted narrowly by the ECJ.

Public lending right

Authors are entitled to compensation where their works are loaned by public libraries in order to compensate them for lost revenue from sales (see the Public Lending Rights Act 1979). The right is administered via a Public Lending Rights Scheme. It is also worth noting that in copyright, much administration of the rights is carried out by organisations known as Collecting Societies.

9. DESIGN LAW

INTRODUCTION

Designs are protected via a combination of a system of registered designs under the Registered Designs Act 1949 (as amended) and design right, with a residual role for copyright (both of the latter are governed by the CDPA 1988).

Design law—a brief history

The UK design regime makes little sense without some knowledge of how the present system evolved. Traditionally, copyright was an important source of protection in the design field, but a separate system of registered design was also developed to protect aesthetic designs. Before the late 1980s, there was the choice of applying (and paying for) a registered design, or relying on copyright (which had less stringent requirements, subsisted automatically and had a longer term of protection); in such circumstances it is unsurprising that copyright was favoured. However, in some cases, *e.g. Dorling v Honnor Marine* (1964), copyright was abused in the design field in relation to non-aesthetic designs. In *British Leyland v Armstrong* (1986), the courts were reduced to relying on a non-IP concept, that of non-derogation from grant, to prevent copyright in spare car parts being used to develop a *de facto* monopoly in such parts.

The result was a raft of reforms in the late 1980s, which saw some reform of registered designs, the cutting back of the role of copyright in the design field and, in its place, the introduction of a new IPR for designs—the design right. More recently, in response to European developments, further reforms were introduced in 2001 to expand the registered design regime.

UK and EU design law

As noted above, in the UK designs are governed by both the RDA 1949 and the CDPA 1988. The RDA 1949 was amended in December 2001 so as to implement the Designs Directive (98/71/EC). An application for a national registered design may be made to the Design Registry (part of the UK Patent Office), but it is also possible to apply for Registered Community Designs (RCDs). Further, national unregistered designs (known as design rights) may subsist in the UK under the CDPA 1988, but there is also a very different Community unregistered right—the Unregistered Community Design (the UCD). RCDs and UCDs (which can exist both in the absence of or in parallel with registered or unregistered rights under national design law) are valid in the entire EU and are governed by the Community Design Regulation (No. 6/2002 of December 12, 2001). Applications for RCDs are considered by OHIM.

Although IP law courses tend to focus on UK law, and therefore the provisions of the RDA 1949 and the CDPA 1988, the student should be aware of the existence of these community design rights. Further, it is expected that ECJ jurisprudence on the designs directive will have an increasing effect on UK design law, so students should therefore be prepared to refer to provisions of the directive. Hereafter, this text only refers to the UK design regime.

The routes to protecting a design

Today, therefore, a design may be protected in the UK by one, or more, of the following:

(a) The design right (CDPA 1988, ss.213–264 (Part III)).
(b) Registered designs (Registered Designs Act 1949, as amended. Hereafter referred to as RDA 1949).
(c) Copyright, often termed "artistic copyright" (CDPA 1988, s.51–53).

The design right and registered design systems are set out below and the role of copyright in the design sphere is also briefly summarised.

THE DESIGN RIGHT

Introduction

The unregistered design right (the design right) was originally introduced to extend protection to functional designs (although it should be noted that the new registered design regime now also has a role in the protection of functional designs, see below). Design rights will automatically subsist in *both* functional and aesthetic designs, where there is:

(a) A design (as per CDPA 1988, s.213(2), any aspect of the shape or configuration, internal or external of the whole or part of an article);

(b) Qualification of the design (CDPA 1988, ss.213(5) and 217–221);

(c) Originality (*i.e.* not commonplace in the design field in question at the time of creation (CDPA 1988, s.213(4));

(d) The design must be recorded (CDPA 1988, s.213(6)); and

(e) The design is not excluded design, *i.e.*

  (ii) Not a method or principle of construction (CDPA 1988, s.213(3)(a));

  (iii) Not a "must fit" feature of shape or configuration (CDPA 1988, s.213(3)(b)(i));

  (iv) Not a "must match" feature of shape or configuration (CDPA 1988, s.213(3)(b)(ii));

  (v) Not a surface decoration (CDPA 1988, s.213(3)(c)).

A "design"

This is defined as "the design of any aspect of the shape or configuration (internal or external) of the whole or part of an article" (CDPA 1988, s.213(2)). This means that the shape of an article (*Fulton Co. Ltd v Grant Barnett & Co* (2000)) or its configuration, *i.e.* the way in which an article fits together (*Electronic Techniques v Critchley* (1997)), may be protected in respect of the whole article or its constituent parts. The features of an article that are protected may be invisible to the human eye (*Ocular Sciences v Aspect Vision Care* (1997)).

Qualification

As per CDPA 1988, ss.217–221, the design must qualify for protection via a "qualifying person" (a person who is a citizen or subject of a qualifying country or a person who is domiciled in a qualifying country). This person could be the designer, the commissioner of the design, the employer of the designer or the first person to market the design.

Originality

A design is not original if it is commonplace in the design field in question at the time of its creation (CDPA 1988, s.213(4)). The leading case here is *Farmer's Build Limited v Carrier Bulk Materials Handling Limited* (1999), where it was commented that a design had to be original in the sense that it is the independent work of the designer. The court set out a restrictive approach to the concept of "commonplace", but made it clear that it is not a test of novelty. In deciding whether the design of an article is commonplace, and therefore not original, the following should be noted:

(i) The design must not have been copied from the design of an earlier article.

(ii) The design should be *compared* with the design of contemporaneous articles produced by other parties *in the same field*, in order to ascertain similarities. This comparative exercise must be conducted objectively and in the light of the evidence, including evidence from experts in the relevant field.

(iii) This comparison is one of fact and degree. The closer the similarity of the various designs, the more likely it is that the design is commonplace. However, where aspects of the claimant's design are only to be found in the defendant's design, the court is entitled to conclude that the design in question is not commonplace.

Recordal

For the design right to subsist, the design must be recorded either as a model or as a design document. Oral disclosure of the design, therefore, would be insufficient.

Exclusions

The following are excluded from the ambit of the design right:

(i) Methods or principles of construction (CDPA 1988, s.213(3)(a)). Design rights do not subsist in methods or principle of construction.

(ii) "Must fit" designs are excluded, *i.e.* design rights will not subsist in "features of shape or configuration of an article which enable the article to be connected to, placed in, around or against, another article so that either article can perform its function" (CDPA 1988, s.213(3)(b)(i)). Hence, design features that allow the article to interface, link, connect or otherwise physically relate to another article are excluded. "Must fit" has been held to extend to features that relate to the human body, such as contact lenses (*Ocular Science v Aspect Vision Care* (1997)). A plug that is to interface with a socket would also be caught (*Amoena v Trulife* (1995)). See also *Dyson Ltd v Qualtex Ltd* (2004).

(iii) "Must match" designs are excluded, *i.e.* design rights will not subsist in "features of shape or configuration which are dependent upon the appearance of another article of which the article is intended by the designer to form an integral part" (CDPA 1988, s.213(3)(b)(ii)). Therefore, any features which need to be made in a certain way for aesthetic reasons will be excluded (*e.g.* see *Mark Wilkinson Furniture v Woodcraft Designs* (1998). See also *Dyson Ltd v Qualtex Ltd* (2004)). Car body panels would also be excluded under "must match".

(iv) Surface decoration (CDPA 1988, s.213(3)(c)). Design rights do not subsist in surface decoration such as a paint finish or beading on the surface of an article (*Mark Wilkinson Furniture v Woodcraft Designs* (1998)).

The "must fit" and "must match" exclusions were primarily intended to limit the registration of spare parts. "Must fit" related to functional considerations and "must match" is an aesthetic version of the "must fit" exclusion.

Ownership

The designer is the first owner of an unregistered design (CDPA 1988, s.215(1)) unless:

(i) The design was commissioned. Here the commissioner is the first owner (CDPA 1988, s.215(2)).
(ii) The design was made in the course of employment. Here the employer is the first owner (CDPA 1988, s.215(3)).
(iii) Where the design right subsists via qualification with reference to the first marketer of the design, that person is the first owner (CDPA 1988, s.215(4)).

Rights of the design right owner

The design right owner has the exclusive right to reproduce (copy) the design for commercial purposes by making articles to the design or making design documents (CDPA 1988, s.226(1)).

In the context of design rights, CDPA 1988, s.226(2) requires that copying be proved (*e.g.* see *Amoena v Trulife* (1995)). The allegedly infringing article (or design document) is to be made the same, or be *substantially the same*, to the protected design. This is an objective test to be decided by the judge through the eyes of the person to whom the design is directed (*CH Engineering v Klucznic* (1992)).

Primary Infringement

It constitutes infringement for any person to engage in the following for commercial purposes (or to purport to authorise such activity) without the permission of the design right owner (CDPA 1988, s.226):

(i) To copy the design; and
(ii) Then produce articles or design documents that are identical or substantially similar (see *L Woolley Jewellers v A & A Jewellers* (2003)) to the design.

Secondary Infringement

Secondary infringement occurs where, without the permission of the design right owner, infringing articles are imported or dealt with (*e.g.* selling infringing articles), where that person knows or has reason to believe that the article is infringing (CDPA 1988, s.227(1)).

Exceptions

The following exceptions to infringement are provided:

  (i) Where copyright subsists in a work in which a design right also subsists, it is not an infringement of the design right to do anything that constitutes copyright infringement in the work (CDPA 1988, s.236).
 (ii) Any person is entitled to a license of right in the last five years of the design right (CDPA 1988, s.237).
(iii) There is a specific provision for Crown use of designs (CDPA 1988, s.240).

Duration of the design right

The design right subsists from the date upon which the design is recorded or an article is made to the design (CDPA 1988, s.213(6)). Where an article made to the design is sold within five years of the end of the first calendar year from that date, the right will subsist for 10 years from the end of the year of first marketing (CDPA 1988, s.216(1)(b)). Otherwise, the right endures for 15 years from the date on which the design is recorded in a design document or in an article (CDPA 1988, s.216(1)(a)).

During the final five years, "licenses of right" may be available to third parties (CDPA 1988, ss.237–239).

Remedies

Remedies are discussed in general in Chapter 2. The following remedies are available for design right infringement:

  (i) Damages (CDPA 1988, s.229(2)), but damages are not available against an innocent primary infringer (CDPA 1988, s.233), and against the innocent secondary infringer only damages of a reasonable royalty may be awarded (CDPA 1988, s.233). However, additional damages are also available (CDPA 1988, s.229(3)).
 (ii) Injunctions (CDPA 1988, s.229(2)).
(iii) Account of profits (CDPA 1988, s.229(2)).
 (iv) An order for delivery up (CDPA 1988, s.230).
  (v) An order for disposal (CDPA 1988, s.231).
 (vi) There is a provision for groundless threat of infringement proceedings (CDPA 1988, s.253).

REGISTERED DESIGNS

Introduction

As noted above, the registered designs regime underwent substantial reform in December 2001 in order to implement the Directive on the Legal Protection of Designs (Directive 98/71/EC). The Directive is intended to harmonise the laws of EU member states and it paves the way for further Community design harmonisation. Students should note that much of the pre-December 2001 caselaw on the RDA 1949 is no longer relevant to designs registered under the current regime.

The following may be registered under the RDA 1949:

(a) A "design" (as per RDA 1949, s.1(2), which refers to various aspects of the appearance of the whole or part of a product);
(b) That is novel (RDA 1949, ss.1(A)(2) and 1(B)(1),(2), (5) and (6));
(c) That has individual character (RDA 1949, s.1B(1)(3) and (4)); and
(d) Does not fall into any of the exceptions to registration:
  (i) Is not a component part of a "complex product" (RDA 1949, s.1(3)) that is not visible during normal use (RDA 1949, s.1B(8));
  (ii) Is not a feature solely dictated by technical function (RDA 1949, s.1C(1));
  (iii) Is not a "must fit" design (RDA 1949, s.1C(2) and (3));
  (iv) Is not a design contrary to public policy or the accepted principles of morality (RDA 1949, s.1D).

How has the law changed?

Key changes have been made to validity, with the effect that there is a vast increase in the number of things that are registrable. For example, as graphic symbols are now registrable, greater interplay between the law of registered designs and trade mark law can be envisaged, although prior trade marks cannot, of course, be registered as designs. Stricter registration requirements, such a more stringent definition of novelty, have been introduced. The introduction of a 12-month grace period and the reform of infringement (to the advantage of the proprietor of a registered design) are other features of the new regime, with the result that registered design protection, previously rather neglected in practice, is now a very attractive option. As the UK Patent Office has indicated that it will continue with its previous practice of not examining applications with reference to prior art, this means that registered designs potentially offer a speedy and inexpensive form of protection to a wide range of products.

The old regime will continue to apply to all registrations and pending applications existing before December 9, 2001 ("pre-2001 registered designs"), but the new law will apply to the scope of registration and to infringement. However, acts that would not have constituted infringement under the old law will still be permitted in relation to such pre-2001 designs.

Hereafter, this chapter refers to the new registered design regime only. Our understanding of this new regime will increase over the next few years as case law develops. Also, there is likely to be an increasing European influence as a Community designs regime develops.

"Design"

The RDA 1949 defines a design as "the *appearance* of the *whole or part* of a *product* resulting from the features of, in particular, the lines, contours, colours, shape, texture or materials of the product or its ornamentation" (RDA 1949, s.1(2)). *Any* aspect of the appearance of a product (or the entire product) is, therefore, potentially registrable. Aesthetic designs are clearly protectable, but functional designs will also be protected provided that they are not *solely* dictated by technical function (RDA 1949, s.1C(1)).

"Product" is defined as "any industrial or handicraft item *other than a computer program*". The definition includes get up and packaging and, more significantly, graphic symbols and typefaces (RDA 1949, s.1(3)). This means that:

(i) Handicraft items, such as craft jewellery, will now be eligible for registration.

(ii) Significantly, the Act specifically expands protection to include graphic symbols. This means that graphic works, for example logos and character drawings, may be registrable. Potentially, trade marks could be registered as designs as a prelude to trade mark registration. Also, there is now potentially an enforceable right for character merchandising.

(iii) Protection is specifically extended to get up, packaging and typefaces.

(iv) While computer programs not registrable, aspects of the appearance of computer programs, such as computer icons, may well be (see *Apple Computer Inc v Design Registry* (2001), which although decided under the old Act, makes this clear).

Novelty

RDA 1949, s.1B provides that a design is new if no identical design or those differing only in immaterial details has been made available to the public before the date of the application for the registered design (RDA, 1949, s.1A(3)). The novelty rule takes the form of a qualified type of global novelty (RDA 1949, ss.1(B)(5) and (6)); a design is novel where, at the application date, it could not have been known to commercial persons in the European Economic Area, specialising in the relevant sector. This is subject to a 12-month grace period (RDA 1949, s.1B(6)(d)). Some guidance on the approach to novelty has been provided by OHIM (*e.g.* see *Application of Jose Mallent Castello* (2004) and *Application of Leng-D'Or SA* (2005)).

Individual character

In addition to novelty, a design must have individual character (RDA 1949, s.1B). A design will be considered to have individual character if "the overall impression it produces on the informed user differs from the overall impression produced on a user by an earlier design" (RDA 1949, s.1B(3)). In assessing whether the design has this quality, the degree of freedom of the designer in developing the design is to be taken into consideration (RDA 1949, s.1B(4)). Some guidance on the approach to the requirement of individual character has been provided by OHIM (*e.g.* see *Application of Jose Mallent Castello* (2004) and *Application of Leng-D'Or SA* (2005)).

Exceptions to registration

The main exceptions are as follows:

(a) Component parts of a complex product that are not visible during normal use may not be registered (RDA 1949,

s.1B(8)). "Complex product" is defined in RDA 1949, s.1(3)
as "a product composed of at least two replaceable parts
permitting the dis-assembly and re-assembly of the product". In effect, s.1B(8) provides that spare parts not
visible during normal use (*e.g.* car engine parts) are not
registrable, but those which are visible during normal use
(*e.g.* car panels or bumpers) may be registered;

(b) Features that are solely dictated by technical function are
not registrable (RDA 1949, s.1C(1)). Purely functional
designs are, therefore, not registrable;

(c) "Must fit" designs are not registrable. This is a limited
"must fit" provision, similar to, but not the same as that
for the design right. In registered designs "features of
shape that are required for the product in which the
design is incorporated or to which it is applied to be
mechanically connected to or placed in, around or against,
another product so that either product may perform its
function" may not be registered (RDA 1949, s.1C(2)). This
exclusion does not extend to modular systems, *e.g.* stack-
ing chairs or Lego bricks (RDA 1949, s.1C(3)); and

(d) Designs contrary to public policy or the accepted principles of morality are not registrable (RDA 1949, s.1D).

Ownership

The designer is the first owner of a registered design, unless the
design was commissioned, in which case the commissioner is the
first owner, or created in the course of employment, here the
employer would be the first owner (RDA 1949, s.2).

Cancellation of registrations

A registered design may be cancelled by the registrar upon the
successful application for a declaration of invalidity (RDA 1949,
s.11). Any person may make an application for a declaration of
invalidity (RDA 1949, s.11ZB) and the grounds for invalidity
include:

(i) The design does not satisfy one or more of the requirements of RDA 1949, s.1A(1)(a) or (b), *i.e.* there is not a
novel design with individual character, or it is a design
dictated by technical function, a "must fit" design, or a
design contrary to public policy or immorality.

(ii) It is a design excluded by RDA 1949, Sch.A1 (*e.g.* a registration will be cancelled where the design utilises, without consent, devices or emblems connected to royalty or the Olympic symbol).

(iii) It is caught by the provisions relating to prior trade mark rights or copyright (RDA 1949, s.11A(3) and (4)).

Rights of the registered design owner

The proprietor of a registered design has the exclusive right to use the design, or any design which does not produce on the informed user a different overall impression (RDA 1949, s.7), *i.e. any product* incorporating a registered design may infringe the registration and it is irrelevant as to whether the infringer has copied the registered design.

"Use" covers a wide range of scenarios, including importing or stocking a product made to the design (see RDA 1949, s.7(2)).

Infringement

Once granted, protection begins on the date of filing (RDA 1949, ss.3C(1), 7(6) and 8(1)) and is renewable every five years up to 25 years (RDA 1949, s.8).

A registered design will be infringed where (RDA 1949, s.7A) a person carries out any of the rights exclusive to the registered proprietor (see above), without the consent of the proprietor.

Exceptions

Exceptions to infringement include:

(i) Private and non-commercial use of the design (RDA 1949, s.7A(2)(a)).

(ii) Experimental use of the design (RDA 1949, s.7A(2)(b)).

(iii) Reproducing the design for teaching purposes, subject to some qualifications (RDA 1949, s.7A(2)(c)).

(iv) There are specific exclusions relating to ships or aircraft registered in a third country but temporarily in the UK (RDA 1949, s.7A(2)(d)–(f)).

(v) Exhaustion within the EEA (RDA 1949, s.7A(4)).

(vi) Certain acts relating to spare parts, see "The protection of spare parts", below (RDA 1949, s.7A(5)).

(vii) No proceedings may be brought for acts committed before the grant of the certificate of registration (RDA 1949, s.7(6)).

(viii) Crown use of the design (RDA 1949, s.12).

The protection of spare parts

The issue of spare parts has bedevilled design law for some time (*e.g.* see *British Leyland v Armstrong* (1986)) and has not yet been the subject of European harmonisation. Under the Directive, however, the Commission was obliged to commission a report on the spare parts issue at the end of 2004, and the Commission has proposed amendments to the design regulation in relation to spare parts. If the directive is amended, the RDA 1949 is likely to require further reform on the issue of spare parts.

In the current UK law there is some scope for the protection of spare parts as registered designs. Importantly, while there is a "must fit" exclusion (RDA 1949, s.1C(2) and (3)), there is no "must match" exclusion in registered design law, but this is mitigated by the fact that there is no protection for spare parts used to restore appearance (RDA 1949, s.7A(5)), so while such parts could be registered, they cannot be enforced. This (along with exclusions from registrability relating to "complex product" in RDA 1949, s.1B(8) and the exclusion of purely functional designs by RDA 1949, s.1C(1) should help limit proprietors' ability to use registered design law to establish a monopoly in spare parts.

Remedies

Remedies are discussed in general in Chapter 2, most of the remedies discussed in that chapter should be available for registered design infringement, including:

(i) Damages. However, no damages may be awarded against the innocent infringer (RDA 1949, s.9).

(ii) Injunctions.

(iii) Account of profits.

(iv) There is a provision for groundless threat of infringement (RDA 1949, s.26).

ARTISTIC COPYRIGHT

Scope of protection

In effect, only original design articles and design documents may be protected by copyright law as artistic works (*e.g.* as sculptures or works of artistic craftsmanship). You should refer to Chapters 7 and 8 for general information about copyright law, this section only refers to provisions specific to copyright in the design field.

CDPA 1988, ss.51–52 limits the role of copyright in the design field. Copyright will not subsist in the following:

(i) Articles and design documents other than artistic works (CDPA 1988, 51(1)); and

(ii) Where an article is made to the design/copy article made from design (CDPA 1988, s.51). See *Lambretta v Next & Teddy Smith* (2005).

The duration of copyright in the design field may be limited (CDPA 1988, s.52), being:

(i) Life of the author plus 70 years; or

(ii) Where the design is applied industrially (*i.e.* more than 50 copies are made) the copyright term in the industrial design field is limited to 25 years from the date of first marketing. Some things are excluded from this (CDPA 1988, s.52(4)(b)) and therefore attract the full copyright term of life plus 70 years, such as sculptures, medals and printed matter of primarily an artistic or literary character.

---

10. EXAMINATION CHECKLIST

N.B. These questions generally follow the order in which topics appear in this book. But not all of them do. In particular, some issues may require discussion of more than one IPR, e.g. patent questions may involve breach of confidence issues and trade mark issues might also require consideration of passing off.

1. What rights are included in the concept of "intellectual property law"?
2. What non-pecuniary remedies are available for IP infringement?
3. What is meant by "account of profits"?
4. On what basis is an account calculated?
5. What is the rule as to availability of damages?
6. Damages and account of profits are examples of pecuniary final remedies; list the non-pecuniary final remedies.
7. What is a Norwich Pharmacal Order?
8. How is *Microsoft v Plato* (1999) significant in respect of final injunctions?
9. What is the test for the availability of an interim injunction? How does this test differ in breach of confidence cases where there are issues as to freedom of expression?
10. There are two remedies available in proceedings without notice that are particularly useful in IP law, what are these and on what grounds are they available?
11. What criminal sanctions are available for IP infringement?
12. What is meant by a "threats action"?
13. The PA 1977 sets out the substantive criteria of patentability, what are these?
14. What things are not *inventions "as such"*?
15. The concept of "technical effect" is important in what part of patent law? Explain what this concept is and how it is used.
16. Are business methods patentable?
17. What is meant by a non-patentable invention?
18. What does *anticipation* mean?
19. What is the novelty test?
20. What is the "priority date" and why is it significant in the patent system?
21. Some new uses can still be novel. What are these new uses and what authority is there for their being novel?
22. What does *non-obviousness* mean?
23. The "skilled man" is relevant to obviousness—how? And what are his attributes?
24. What is the statutory test for inventive step? What is the significance of the *Windsurfer* test in this contest?
25. So-called secondary considerations are relevant to obviousness. Explain how this is the case and give examples of secondary considerations.
26. Discuss what is meant by *industrial application*.

27. To whom may a patent be granted?
28. Can employee inventors own inventions made during the course of employment?
29. Can employee inventors be compensated?
30. "Sufficiency" is an important concept in patent law. What does it mean?
31. List the acts that constitute patent infringement.
32. Are there any exceptions to infringement?
33. On what grounds may a patent be revoked?
34. Claim interpretation is a key element of patent infringement. Explain what is meant by "claim interpretation". Why is it important and what is the significance of *Wheatly v Drillsafe* (2001)?
35. What remedies are available for patent infringement?
36. What impact has the Human Rights Act 1998 had on breach of confidence?
37. *Coco v Clarke* (1969) is a significant breach of confidence case—why?
38. What constitutes information with the *necessary quality of confidence*?
39. What circumstances give rise to an *obligation of confidence*?
40. The position of the current employee differs from that of the ex-employee when it comes to implying an obligation of confidence. What is the difference between current and ex-employees in this area?
41. Are third parties who receive confidential information bound by an obligation of confidence?
42. What constitutes *use of confidential information*?
43. Is intent relevant in relation to the concept of "use" in breach of confidence?
44. Subconscious use does not breach the obligation of confidence—true or false?
45. What defences are available against an action for breach of confidence?
46. What remedies are available for an action for breach of confidence?
47. What is the function of a trade mark? What are collective and certification marks and how do they differ from ordinary trade marks?
48. *Absolute grounds for refusal* are concerned with a conflict based on third party rights—true or false?
49. *Relative grounds for refusal* are concerned with objections based on the mark itself—true or false?

50. What is the Nice Agreement?
51. Define a "trade mark".
52. Set out the absolute and relative grounds for refusal.
53. Is it possible to graphically represent a scent mark? What criteria are used in determining whether graphic representation is adequate?
54. There is a proviso to TMA 1994, s.3(1). What is it? Why is it significant?
55. Explain what a mark devoid of distinctive character is.
56. How would you describe an exclusively descriptive sign?
57. What is meant by a generic sign?
58. The TMA 1994 has special provisions for shape marks. What are these and how is *Philips v Remington* (2002) significant?
59. When will a trade mark be immoral?
60. What constitutes a deceptive mark?
61. What is an "earlier trade mark"?
62. What is the scope of "honest concurrent use"?
63. What constitutes an "identical mark"?
64. The concept of confusing similarity is important both to the relative grounds for refusal (*i.e.* TMA 1994, s.5(2)), but also to infringement (*i.e.* TMA 1994, s.10(2)). What does "confusion" mean? Does "confusion" mean the same thing as "association"?
65. When will conflict with a mark of repute be a valid ground upon which to refuse registration?
66. On what grounds may a mark be revoked?
67. What acts constitute trade mark infringement?
68. Some defences to trade mark infringement are available. What are they?
69. What remedies are available for trade mark infringement?
70. Certain criminal offences are relevant to trade mark law— what are these?
71. What are the elements for the action of passing off as set out in *Jif Lemon* (1990)? Is there an alternative formulation? Which do you prefer?
72. How would you define "goodwill"? Why are territorial considerations important?
73. What actions might constitute an actionable misrepresentation in passing off?
74. Various forms of damage may result from the misrepresentation; list these.
75. What defences and remedies are available to an action of passing off?

76. What is the main UK authority on cybersquatting?
77. Is passing off helpful in endorsement, sponsorship or character merchandising?
78. Is deception required for a successful action in passing off?
79. The CDPA 1988 sets out the conditions that have to be satisfied before copyright will subsist, what are these?
80. List the primary copyright works.
81. List the secondary copyright works.
82. Describe the significance of *Norowzian v Arks (No.2)* (1999).
83. What role (if any) does artistic merit have for artistic works?
84. What is the test used to determine whether a work is a work of artistic craftsmanship?
85. Identify the copyright works that subsist in the following: the website of a national newspaper, a CD compilation of popular songs, an episode of a BBC soap opera, a cartoon and the soundtrack of a Hollywood movie. Please bear in mind that multiple copyrights may subsist in any one "real world" object.
86. What is meant by "the idea/expression dichotomy"?
87. Which copyright works must be original? What is meant by an "original work"?
88. Is there a statutory standard of originality?
89. Artistic works are subject to the requirement of fixation—true or false?
90. Who is the author of a copyright work?
91. Who is the first owner of a copyright work?
92. When will joint ownership of a copyright work occur?
93. When is an employer the first owner of copyright?
94. What are the two forms of copyright infringement?
95. What are the exclusive rights of the copyright owner?
96. What does "taking the whole or a substantial part" of a work mean and why is this requirement significant?
97. Define what acts constitute infringement of the reproduction right.
98. What acts constitute secondary infringement?
99. Set out the main "permitted acts".
100. Fair dealing in a copyright work is allowed for any purpose—true or false?
101. If a film-maker deliberately includes a musical work in his film, this will not constitute copyright infringement because of the provisions on incidental inclusion—true or false?

102. Decompiling a computer program can not constitute copyright infringement—true or false?
103. What remedies are available for copyright infringement?
104. What are moral rights?
105. Give the duration of copyright in the following works: a computer-generated picture, the typography of a literary work in which (literary) copyright has lapsed, an unreleased sound recording that was made in 1973, and a film.
106. Which IPRs are relevant in the design field? Which IP statutes are relevant?
107. When will the design right subsist?
108. Define a "design" under the design right legislation.
109. When will a design qualify for design right protection?
110. What is meant by "originality" in the context of design rights? (You might also consider how it differs to the originality requirement in copyright law.)
111. Explain the main exclusions from the design right. In particular, what is meant by "must fit" and "must match"?
112. Explain the ownership rules for unregistered designs.
113. What constitutes infringement of the design right? What are the exceptions to infringement?
114. What is the duration of the design right?
115. What remedies are available for design right infringement?
116. What are the registrability requirements for registered designs?
117. Are the following "designs" within the meaning of the RDA 1949: A cartoon character, grooves on a milk container, computer icons and a handmade earring?
118. What is meant by "novelty" under the RDA 1949? (You might also consider how it differs to novelty in patent law.)
119. When will a design have "individual character" under the RDA 1949?
120. Explain the main exceptions to registration under the RDA 1949, in particular, explaining the "must fit" exclusion.
121. What acts constitute infringement of a registered design? What are the exceptions to infringement (in particular, explain RDA 1949, s.7A(5))?
122. What would be the duration of copyright in an industrially applied design?

11. SAMPLE QUESTIONS AND MODEL ANSWERS

THE EXAMINATION

The golden rule for most law examinations would be to "answer the *question; all* of the question (*i.e.* all its constituent parts) and *nothing but* the question (*i.e.* do not digress, keep your answer relevant to the question)". Preparation, revision, practice and planning all have a role in this.

Preparation

Most IP examinations require candidates to answer problem and essay questions. The format and style of examinations and the rubric, of course, varies between institutions, as may the syllabus. Students are strongly advised to study their course syllabus and any relevant examination regulations.

If possible, obtain and study past papers. The purpose of this is not to facilitate "question spotting" (a dangerous practice, as past papers cannot be regarded as providing an accurate guide to questions that will be included in the forthcoming examination), but rather to ensure that you are familiar with the format and style of the examination, and in order to facilitate practice (see below).

Revision

By now you should be aware of the revision methods that you find to be most effective. Students should try to ensure that they have adequate time for revision.

Practice

Too many candidates make the mistake of revising, revising and revising, and the first time they attempt to apply their hard-won knowledge and understanding is in the examination. As most IP examinations assess your ability to analyse and discuss issues within a limited period of time, it makes sense to practice this skill as part of your revision by answering questions from past papers. If you do this in good time, your course lecturer or tutor may be prepared to mark or comment on your practice answers.

Planning

During the examination, it is often advisable to plan your answers. Planning is conducive to structured and clear work.

Citing case law and EPO decisions

A practical matter; some of the IP cases have long and complicated names that might be difficult to remember in a closed-book examination. Naturally you should follow your institution's referencing protocols in coursework and should cite cases fully, but in examinations the rules are likely to be more flexible. Although you **must** check with your course lecturer or tutor as to what is acceptable in your institution, the following practices are usually acceptable in IP examinations: referring to UK and ECJ trade mark cases by the mark (as there is a trade mark convention that word marks should be capitalised, this means that you should, for example, refer to the *TREAT* (not Treat) case for *British Sugar v James Robinson* (1996)) and to EPO decisions by part of name of decision (perhaps "the Picture-retrieval EPO decision" rather than *Koninklijke Philip's Electronics/Picture-retrieval system*. Or *Eisai* for *EISAI/Second medical indication* (1985)).

In coursework, of course, all such material must be fully cited. As with a law exam in any subject, if you forget the name of an important case, it is better to briefly describe the facts and findings of the case instead, rather than saying nothing.

ESSAY QUESTIONS

The main function of essay questions in law exams is to test the depth of a candidate's *understanding* of the law. Therefore, a good answer to an essay question will address the question directly and, in addition to providing an accurate description of the relevant law, will engage in critical analysis; *i.e.* the candidate will not only set out what the law *is* but will indicate what the law *should be*. Critical analysis usually involves discussion of aspects of the law that are successful and aspects that are problematic—often it is also helpful if the candidate goes on to indicate, briefly, how the law could be reformed. Essay questions can often be answered in different ways, depending on the candidate's views. Nevertheless, it is helpful to consider the merits of opposing views, and throughout your answer you must make reference to authority and, for the statutory IPRs, the relevant statutory provisions. Pay some attention to the structure of your answer; it is surprising how many candidates in exam conditions forget that essays should have a beginning (a short introduction) a middle (what the relevant law is, relevant arguments and critical analysis) and an end (a conclusion).

Sample question

"Morality and public policy have no role to play in the patent system." Discuss.

Sample answer

This is an essay question that could, potentially, be answered in a wide range of ways and the topic can generate very strong views. Nevertheless, candidates should be wary of writing an answer with "too much opinion and not enough law". The starting point should be the PA 1977, s.1(3), which provides that where the commercial exploitation of an invention is contrary to public policy or morality, the invention is unpatentable, so morality clearly has *some* role to play in the patent system. However, that role may be a very small one, depending on one's interpretation of the relevant jurisprudence. There is little modern UK case law in this area, but there are a number of decisions of the EPO (so you should critically discuss relevant EPO decisions such as *Harvard OncoMouse* (1990) and *PLANT GENETIC SYSTEMS/Glutamine Synthetase Inhibitors* (1995)), and the question remains: *should* there be a role in the patent system for public policy considerations and morality?

Candidates would also be expected to critically discuss the provisions pertaining to morality in PA 1977, Sch.A2, *e.g.* should human germ line therapy be excluded? Do the provisions relating to plant and animal varieties set out a reasonable position (see *NOVARTIS/Transgenic plant* (1999) and *Harvard Onco-Mouse* (1990))? Schedule A2 implements the Directive on the Legal Protection of Biotechnological Inventions (98/44/EC) into UK law and this directive, in effect, harmonises EPO jurisprudence relating to the moral and public policy concerns in relation to biotechnological inventions. Although discussion of these biotechnological aspects is relevant, the candidate should be wary; the essay question is not *limited* to biotechnological inventions, so the candidate should ensure that they spend sufficient time in their answer describing and analysing general EPO and UK jurisprudence on morality and public policy.

It is difficult to be prescriptive as to how candidates might approach their analysis of EPO jurisprudence on these issues, as so much depends on the individual candidate's opinion. Certainly he/she should consider discussing the moral aspects relating to the patentability of biotechnological inventions and the patentability of plant and animal varieties, but the main emphasis should be on analysis of the jurisprudence on morality and public policy.

Following this analysis, candidates should conclude by coming to some view as to the extent that morals and public policy considerations will be considered in the UK patent process. If they disagree with this position, candidates might also (briefly) set out recommendations for reform.

PROBLEM QUESTIONS

The main function of problem questions in law exams is to test the candidate's ability to *apply* the law. There is little or no scope to discuss what the law should be; the candidate should direct their efforts to applying the law and going on to *advise* the party or parties in the question as to their rights and remedies (if any). Problem questions largely dictate the structure of answers, for example you can structure your answer by issue or by party, as appropriate. A useful rule of thumb in planning an answer to a problem question is to question the significance of all the information provided in the question. Unless your examiner is fond of red herrings, it is likely that descriptions, events, dates, actions etc., are all relevant.

Sample question

James is a stand-up comedian with a talent for improvisation. As part of his act, he asks the audience for themes and styles for songs which he then improvises; he sings and accompanies himself on a piano. When James is performing at the StarStruck Club, the owner of the club allows two members of the audience,

Gill and Grant, to record James. James does not give permission for this.

Gill and Grant then make 200 copies of James' improvised songs. These are sold to Fidgets, a respectable music shop. Fidgets put the tapes on sale and play one of the tapes over the shop's sound system to encourage customers to purchase it.

One of these customers is Phillip, an aspiring novelist. Philip is so inspired by "Rejection", one of James' improvised songs which describes a blind date gone wrong, that he writes a 500 page novel (called "Rejection") based on the incident as it is described in this two-minute song. This novel is to be published next month. Phillip has called the foolish male protagonist in his novel "James".

Advise James.

Sample answer

This problem question raises a wide range of copyright issues. Relevant case law and statutory authority should be cited in addressing these points, which include:

(a) Do any copyright works subsist in James' performance? Yes, copyright is likely to subsist in James' songs as original literary (CDPA 1988, s.3(1)) and musical (CDPA 1988, s.3(1)(a)) works. Such works must be fixed (CDPA 1988, s.3(2)), but Gill and Grant have fixed the work via their recording (CDPA 1988, s.3(3)). The qualification requirement is also met. Copyright will also subsist in the recording that Gill and Grant have made (but who will own this?). Candidates might also briefly consider the position as to performers' rights.

As suggestions for the songs came from the audience, is James the author of the literary and musical works that subsist in these songs? *Wiseman v George Weidenfeld and Nicholson Ltd and Donaldson* (1985) suggest that merely to supply ideas would be insufficient for members of the audience to be considered as joint authors, and the test suggested in *Cala Homes* (1995) has not been met, so James is probably the author. James is, therefore, likely to be the first owner of the copyrights in the songs (unless he is an employee of the StarStruck Club). If James has not assigned or licensed his rights, he will be able to enforce the economic rights in these works (*i.e.* he will be able to bring proceedings for primary and secondary infringement, as appropriate). In either case, as the author James will also have certain moral rights in relation to these copyright works.

(b) What is the position of the owner of the StarStruck Club? Has the owner authorised Gill and Grant's activities? If so, analysis of *CBS v Amstrad* (1988) is necessary in order to assess whether he/she has authorised infringement (CDPA 1988, s.16(2)). Certainly it seems that he/she knew of Gill and Grant's activities, so the candidate should consider whether the owner's actions fall within CDPA 1988, s.25. Candidates should consider whether the club owner might benefit from any of the permitted acts (this is unlikely) and what remedies (if any) that James may have against the club owner.

(c) What is the position of Gill and Grant? Their activities are likely to constitute a range of primary and secondary infringements. For example, there is infringement of the reproduction right (CDPA 1988, s.17(2)) as well as the distribution right (CDPA 1988, s.18) and public performance rights (s.19). Candidates might refer to cases such as *Ladbroke v William Hill* (1964) and *Infabrics v Jaytex* (1982) in their analysis here. Candidates should also consider the position as to secondary infringement, in particular CDPA 1988, s.23–24, and performers' rights.

Will any of the permitted acts be relevant? Recording without permission and selling these recordings is unlikely to constitute fair dealing for any of the permitted purposes (CDPA 1988, ss.29–30) and no other permitted act appears relevant, for example, the public interest defence does not apply to Gill and Grant's activities. Candidates should therefore consider what remedies might be relevant. James might press for additional damages (CDPA 1988, s.97(2)), as well as a prohibitory injunction to prevent further copies of the songs being made. There may be some scope for criminal sanctions via CDPA 1988, ss.107–8.

(d) The position of the music shop, Fidgets. Candidates should consider any relevant secondary infringements here. The issue of *mens rea* will be crucial to establishing infringement here. Again, any remedies that may be available to James should be noted.

(e) What is the position of Phillip—does Phillip's book

infringe the literary copyright in James' song? Can James prevent Philip from calling the book's main character "James"? In relation to the first question, there is unlikely to be sufficient originality in the title "Rejection" for copyright to subsist (alternatively, one could argue that the *de minimis* principle applies here, as in *Exxon Corporation v Exxon Ind.* (1982)). However, discussion of infringement and the idea–expression dichotomy is germane to the issue of whether a 500-page book based on a two-minute song can constitute infringement of the literary copyright subsisting in that: the "plot" would surely be tantamount to a non-protected idea (*e.g. Green v New Zealand Broadcasting Corporation* (1989)) and it is unlikely to constitute a "substantial taking" (see *Ladbroke v William Hill* (1964), *Hawkes v Paramount Films* (1934) and *Bauman v Fussell* (1953)). Relevant infringements and remedies should be set out. The candidate might also briefly consider whether James can prevent Philip from calling the book's main character "James"—this is unlikely to be possible under copyright law.

12. USEFUL WEBSITES

Although one should be wary of the provenance and quality of internet material on IP matters, there are a number of official websites that provide useful information. A selection of such sites is provided below:

EU MATERIAL

The Europa website (*http://europa.eu.int*) is the official EU website and an important resource, but please note that it is updated regularly and when that happens, the URLs provided below may not work:

(i) *http://europa.eu.int/comm/internal_market/copyright/index_ en.htm* for material on copyright; and

(ii) *http://europa.eu.int/comm/internal_market/indprop/index_
en.htm* for material on enforcement, patents, trade marks
and designs.

In addition, you might explore the IPR Helpdesk website
(*www.ipr-helpdesk.org/controlador.jsp?cuerpo=cuerpo&seccion=
principal&len=en*) for general IP material, the online EPO guidelines (see *www.european-patent-office.org/legal/gui_lines/e/c_iv.htm*)
in order to aid your understanding of patent law and you might
find the OHIM website (*http://oami.eu.int/en/default.htm*) useful if
you wish to learn more about the Community trade mark and
Community design regimes.

UK MATERIAL

The UK Patent Office website (*www.patent.gov.uk/*) is a good
resource to browse for information about the UK patent, trade
mark, copyright and design regimes. Basic introductory information about IP in general can be found at the UK government's
IP website (*www.intellectual-property.gov.uk/*).

INDEX

ACCOUNT OF PROFITS, 5
ADVERTISING,
  comparative, 59–60
AESTHETIC CREATIONS, 14
AQUIESCENCE, 57
ARTISTIC COPYRIGHT, 109
ARTISTIC WORKS, 73–74
AUDITORY SIGNS, 42
AUTHOR,
  employee as, 80–81
  identifying the, 79–80
  joint, 80–81
  more than one, 80–81

BAD FAITH, 51–52
BIOLOGICAL SUBJECT MATTER,
  18–19
BREACH OF CONFIDENCE,
  action for, 32–33
  commercial relationships, 35
  defences, 36
  employment relationships,
    35
  extent of protection, 33
  obligation of confidence,
    34–35
  privacy, right of, 30–32
  quality of confidence,
    33–34
  remedies, 37
  third party recipient,
    35–36
  unauthorised use, 36
BROADCASTS, 75, 76
BUSINESS METHODS, 16

CERTIFICATION MARKS, 39–40
CHARACTER MERCHANDISING, 70
COLLECTIVE MARKS, 39–40
COMPARATIVE ADVERTISING, 59–60
COMPUTER PROGRAMS, 14–15

CONFIDENCE, See BREACH OF
  CONFIDENCE
COPYRIGHT,
  artistic WORKS, 73–74
  author,
    employee as, 80–81
    identifying the, 79–80
    more than one, 80–81
  broadcasts, 75, 76
  categories of, 71
  defences, 88–90
  definition of, 71
  dramatic WORKS, 73
  duration of, 92–94
  electronic rights management
    information, 88
  employee as author, 79, 81
  EU influence, 72
  film, 75
  fixation requirement, 79
  human rights and, 91
  idea/expression dichotomy,
    76–77
  infringement, 81–82
    adaptation right, 86
    authorising, 84
    communication right, 86
    distribution right, 85
    primary, 83–84
    public performance right,
      85
    rental and lending rights,
      85
    reproduction right, 85
    secondary, 86
  joint authors, 80–81
  literary works, 72–73
  neighbouring rights, 94
  moral rights and, 91
    false attribution, 92
    integrity, 92

COPYRIGHT—*cont.*
  moral rights and—*cont.*
    paternity, 91
    privacy, 92
  musical works, 73
  originality, 77–79
    de minimis principle,
      78–79
    standards of, 78
  ownership of, 79, 81
  performers' rights, 94
  public lending right,
    95–96
  qualification, 72
  remedies, 90–91
  restricted acts, 82–83
  sanctions, 90–91
  sound recordings, 74–75
  sui generic database,
    94–95
  tangibility, 79
  technological protection
    measures, 86–87
    circumvention of, 87–88
  typography right, 76
CRIMINAL OFFENCES, 63
CRIMINAL SANCTIONS, 10
CYBERSQUATTING, 69

DAMAGES, 5–6
DATABASE,
  sui generic, 94–95
DECEPTION, 70
DEFENCES, 88–90
DESIGN RIGHT,
  design, coverage of, 98
  duration OF right, 102
  EU, 97
  exclusions, 100
  history of, 96
  infringement,
    exceptions, 102
    primary, 101
    secondary, 101
  originality, 99
  ownership, 100–101
  rights of, 101

DESIGN RIGHT—*cont.*
  qualification, 99
  recordal, 99
  registered designs, *See*
    Registered designs
  remedies, 102
  routes to protecting, 97
  UK, 97
  unregistered, 98
DISCOVERIES, 14
DOMAIN NAMES, 69
DRAMATIC WORKS, 73

ELECTRONIC RIGHTS MANAGEMENT
    INFORMATION, 88
EMBLEMS, 52
EMPLOYEE,
  author, as, 79, 81
  compensation for, 25
  inventor, as, 25
EUROPEAN PATENT CONVENTION,
    12
EX PARTE ORDERS, 9–10
EXAMINATION CHECKLIST, 109–114

FILM, 75
FIXATION REQUIREMENT, 79
FREEZING INJUNCTION, 10

GOODWILL,
  creation of, 65
  definition of, 64–65
  distinctive element, 65–66
  regional considerations,
    66–67
  shared, 67
  territorial considerations, 66
GRAPHIC REPRESENTATION, 41–43

HUMAN RIGHTS LAW, 91

IDEA/EXPRESSION DICHOTOMY,
    76–77
INFORMATION,
  presentation OF, 17
INFRINGEMENT,
  account of profits, 5

INFRINGEMENT—*cont.*
  adaptation right, 86
  authorising, 84
  communication right, 86
  counterclaim, 27
  copyright, 81–86
  damages, 5–6
  distribution right, 85
  establishing, 28
  exceptions to, 27
  injunction, 7
  interim injunctions, 7–9
  non-pecuniary remedies, 6–7
  primary, 83–84
  public performance right, 85
  remedies for, 4–5
  rental and lending rights, 85
  reproduction right, 85
  secondary, 86
  trade marks, 57–60
INJUNCTION, 7
  freezing, 10
  interim, 7–9
INTELLECTUAL PROPERTY,
  European Instruments,
    3–4
  outline of, 2–3
  scope of, 1–2
INVENTION,
  definition of, 13–14
INVENTIVE STEP, 21–22
INVENTOR,
  employee as, 25

LITERARY WORKS, 72–73

MATHEMATICAL MODELS, 14
MENTAL ACTS, 15–16
MORAL RIGHTS, 91
  false attribution, 92
  integrity, 92
  paternity, 91
  privacy, 92
MORALITY,
  contrary to, 17
MUSICAL WORKS, 73

NEIGHBOURING RIGHTS, 94
NICE AGREEMENT, 40
NON-PATENTABLE INVENTIONS, 17
Novel NEW USES, 20–21
NOVELTY, 19–20
  test for, 19–20

ORIGINALITY, 77–79
  de minimis principle,
    78–79
  standards of, 78
OWNERSHIP, 24–25, 79, 81, 106,
    107

PANTONE SYSTEM, 42
PASSING OFF, 63
  character merchandising, 70
  common field of activity,
    67–68
  damage resulting from, 68
  deception, 70
  defences, 68
  domain names, 69
  elements of, 67
  endorsement, 70
  goodwill,
    creation of, 65
    definition of, 64–65
    distinctive element,
      65–66
    regional considerations,
      66–67
    shared, 67
    territorial considerations,
      66
  get-up, protection of, 66
  misrepresentation, 67
  problems with, 70
  remedies, 68–69
  sponsorship, 70
PATENTS,
  aesthetic creations, 14
  biological subject matter,
    18–19
  business methods, 16
  claim interpretation, 28–29
  computer programs, 14–15

PATENTS—*cont.*
  discoveries, 14
  employee inventor, 25
    compensation for, 25
  European Convention, 12
  industrial application, 24
  information, presentation of,
    17
  infringement, 26
    counterclaim, 27
    establishing, 28
    exceptions to, 27
  introduction of, 11
  invention,
    contrary to morality, 17
    contrary to public policy,
      17
    definition of, 13–14
  inventive step, 21–22
  mathematical models, 14
  mental acts, 15–16
  non-patentable inventions,
    17
  novel new uses, 20–21
  novelty, 19–20
    test for, 19–20
  obtaining, 11–14
  ownership of, 24–25
  revocation, claim for, 27
  scheme, rules or methods, 16
  scientific theories, 14
  secondary consideration,
    23–24
  skilled man, 22
  state of the art, 20
  sufficiency, 25–26
  Windsurfer test, 22–23
PERFORMERS' RIGHTS, 94
PUBLIC LENDING RIGHT, 95–96
PUBLIC POLICY,
  contrary to, 17

REGISTERED DESIGNS, 103
  cancellation of registration,
    106–107
  changes to, 103–104
  complex product, 106

REGISTERED DESIGNS—*cont.*
  design, 104–105
  exceptions to, 105–106
  individual character, 105
  infringement, 107
    exceptions to, 107–108
  must fit, 106
  novelty, 105
  ownership, 106
    rights, of, 107
  remedies, 108
  spare parts, protection of,
    108
REMEDIES, 5–11, 29
  account of profits, 5
  breach of confidence, 37
  copyright, 90–91
  criminal sanctions, 10, 29
  damages, 5–6
  design right, 102
  ex parte orders, 9–10
  final, 5
  freezing injunction, 10
  injunctions, 7–9
  interim, 7–10
  inter partes proceedings, 9
  non-pecuniary, 6–7
  passing off, 68–69
  pecuniary, 5–6
  threats, 10–11
REVOCATION, 27

SANCTIONS, 90–91
SCENTS, 43
SCHEME, RULES AND METHODS, 16
SCIENTIFIC THEORIES, 14
SECONDARY CONSIDERATION, 23–24
SIGNS,
  concept of, 41
  not satisfying the
    requirements, 44
  that are exclusively
    descriptive, 46–48
  that are exclusively generic,
    48
SKILLED MAN, 22
SOUND RECORDINGS, 74–75

SPONSORSHIP, 70
SUFFICIENCY, 25–26

TECHNOLOGICAL PROTECTION
    MEASURES, 86–87
  circumvention of, 87–88
TRADE MARKS,
  acquiescence, 57
  auditory signs, 42
  bad faith, applications in,
      51–52
  blurring of, 56
  certification marks, 39–40
  classification of, 40
  collective marks, 39–40
  colours, 42
  comparative advertisement,
      59–60
  conflict with,
    identical goods and
        services, 53
    identical mark, 53
    mark of repute, 55
    similar goods and ser-
        vices, 53–55
    similar mark, 53–55
  contributory infringement,
      59
  criminal offences, 63
  definition of, 40–43
  degree of similarity, 54
  domain names, 69
  earlier rights, conflict with,
      56
  EC law, 37–38
  exhaustion, 62
  function of, 37
  graphic representation,
      41–43
  holograms, 43
  identical marks, test for,
      54
  identical or similar sign, use
      of, 58
  infringement, 57–60
    defences to, 59
    locality defence, 61

TRADE MARKS—*cont.*
  likelihood of association,
      55
  mark of repute, 55–56
  NICE agreement, 40
  objections to registration,
      40
  PANTONE system, 42
  passing off, *See* PASSING OFF
  prohibited marks, 51
  rectification, 57
  refusal,
    absolute grounds for,
        38–39, 44–52
    marks devoid of
        distinctive character,
        44–46
    marks likely to offend
        morals or deceive,
        50–51
    relative grounds for,
        52–56
  Register of,
    errors or omissions in,
        57
  Registry guidance, 42
  remedies, 62–63
  revocation, 56–57
  scents as, 43
  signs,
    concept of, 41
    not satisfying the
        requirements, 44
    that are exclusively
        descriptive, 46–48
    that are exclusively
        generic, 48
  specially protected
      emblems, 52
  surrender, 56
  tarnishing of, 56
  UK law, 37–38
  unregisterable shapes,
      49–50
  use of,
    another mark, 60

TRADE MARKS—*cont.*
  use of—*cont.*
    certain indications, 61
    intended purpose, 61
    own name and address,
      60

TYPOGRAPHY RIGHT, 76

UNAUTHORISED USE, 36
UNREGISTERABLE SHAPES, 49–50
UNREGISTERED DESIGNS, 98

WINDSURFER TEST, 22–23